'I have many fond memories of working with Roy, first with the reserves and then the first team. Roy is a true professional and could always be relied upon. We became colleagues in October 1984, and Roy's knowledge and experience were invaluable to me in those early days as we forged a great working relationship. That quickly became an even greater friendship. Roy is a credit to the club, and one thing is for certain: he is Spurs through and through.'
Doug Livermore

'The only downside to Roy's career as kit manager at Spurs was that he threatened my spot in our very able staff team! But seriously, his dedication and loyalty to his club have shown through over the years and his great personality in good and bad times was always appreciated by myself and the rest of the management team.'
Peter Shreeves

'Roy's dedication and enthusiasm was always visible and nothing was ever too much trouble for our loyal kit man. When I was a player, he was brilliant, and this always carried on until I became part of the management side of the club. Roy is a credit to his profession.'

Ray Clemence

'I promoted Roy to the first team, and it was a decision I never regretted. His loyalty to the team and Tottenham Hotspur Football Club was second to none during my time at Spurs. As such, Roy is recognised throughout the game as a true professional.'

David Pleat

'Roy Reyland has been part of the Tottenham scene almost as long as I can remember. Kit men come and go, but Roy's loyalty and fantastic attitude has become part of the very fabric of White Hart Lane. Nothing was ever too much trouble for him and, what's more, I am very proud to be able to call him a friend.'

John Motson

SHIRTS
SHORTS &
SPURS

FROM GAZZA TO GINOLA –
MY 29 YEARS AS KIT MAN AT THE LANE

SHIRTS SHORTS & SPURS

ROY REYLAND

JOHN BLAKE

Published by John Blake Publishing Ltd,
3 Bramber Court, 2 Bramber Road,
London W14 9PB, England

www.johnblakepublishing.co.uk

First published in hardback in 2010

ISBN: 978 1 84358 283 0

British Library Cataloguing-in-Publication Data:

A catalogue record for this book is available from the British Library.

Design by www.envydesign.co.uk

Printed in the UK by CPI William Clowes Beccles NR34 7TL

1 3 5 7 9 10 8 6 4 2

Papers used by John Blake Publishing are natural, recyclable products made from
wood grown in sustainable forests. The manufacturing processes conform to the
environmental regulations of the country of origin.

Every attempt has been made to contact the relevant copyright holders, but some
were unavailable. We would be grateful if the appropriate people would contact us.

In memory of my nephew Mark Priddy, who, during the writing of this book, tragically passed away from Huntington's Chorea aged just 41.

ACKNOWLEDGEMENTS

I would firstly like to thank my ghostwriter Jeff Maysh for contacting me out of the blue and convincing me to write this book. I would also like to thank my editor John Wordsworth and everyone at John Blake Publishing for taking a lifetime of stories and committing them to paper.

To Rob Segal, for kindly loaning me his Spurs shirt collection for the photograph you see on the cover, but more importantly for being a special friend for so many years. To Bill Nicholson: a true legend who became both a close friend and mentor to me. And a special thank you to my predecessor, Johnny Wallis, for teaching me how to be the best in the business, and how to cope with all types of players from all around the world.

Also a massive thanks is due to my family, who put up with my moods when we lost. And of course, my daughters Vikki and Abbie: I wish I could have been home more during your childhoods. I hope this story explains where I was all the time. Thank you to all my close friends who are massive Spurs fans and who, for their sins, still travel home and away. And a huge thank you must go to my wife Alison, for all her patience and help while I wrote this book, and for tolerating Jeff Maysh twice a week for six months!

A final, big thank you must go to Tottenham Hotspur Football Club for giving me the opportunity to spend 29 years at the club in a working capacity, and giving me the chance to live my dreams.

Roy Reyland, October 2010.

CONTENTS

FOREWORD

BY STEVE PERRYMAN, 2010

Having played 854 games for Tottenham Hotspur, I know more than anyone that there are ups and downs in football. But I also know that Tottenham is a club where everyone is important, from the very bottom of the ladder to the very top. It's that old cliché you hear about tea ladies, but it's true: in the good times everyone's with you, but in football when you go through the rough times you need all those extra people, willing you on.

When the coach pulls out of Tottenham on the way up North to a grim away match, you need to know everyone is right behind you. And that's why my old friend Roy Reyland was more than just a kit man to Spurs. He brought out the best in the team, win or lose. That's why I love the club. So-called 'non-playing staff' are treated as well as the superstars, and they respond in kind. But mark my words, you've still got to be good at your job to survive at Spurs. No one gets along by being a nice fella, and, if there was a pair of boots missing at a big match, Roy would never have lasted his 29 years at the club.

You see, there's an unwritten trust at Tottenham that everyone is trying their best to achieve: to do their own job to the best of their ability. From the coach driver to the centre half to the physio and kit man, when the shit hits the fan, everyone mucks in. And on a tough day you'd rather see a smiling face than a long face, and Roy would always have a joke in his locker, or a story to tell. Always.

People at Tottenham, backroom staff as well as players, are always being reminded by the fans of their responsibility of wearing that famous lily-white shirt. What that shirt stands for is important, more so than at any other club in the world. Tottenham people are proud of their history, they have a respect for the past and cherish those glorious memories and all that goes with it.

When I first got in the team, I inherited the number 11 shirt, just because it became available, from Roger Morgan, I think. When my place in the team became regular, I took the number 8 shirt from Jimmy Greaves, and, although I didn't think about it at the time, I'd taken the shirt from one of the top goal scorers in the world. I quickly got a letter from a young Spurs fan, saying, 'Do you realise you've got Jimmy Greaves' shirt and you never have a shot at goal!' So of course I felt much more comfortable finishing my career in the number 6 shirt, which I hope I made my own.

Speaking as a player who played so many times for

SHIRTS, SHORTS & SPURS

Spurs, for me there was always a danger of things feeling like a routine. I used to like a change, particularly when we got a new style of shirt. If it were a new player, a new manager or even a new shirt, you'd go out desperate to have a good game. For that reason, I used to love going away and playing in the away strip. It just used to make me feel fresh and new.

In the old days we used to play in the classic white shirt, navy shorts, and navy socks. I used to like navy socks, and I especially hated when we played in white socks. I thought any light-coloured socks looked weak, especially white shorts with white socks. I owned sports shops from the age of 19, and we used to sell a white football shirt which with a different cloth badge could become England, Derby or Tottenham. But to me it only ever looked 'right' with the cockerel on the chest.

I remember getting obsessed with the different shades of blue in our kit. At one League Cup Final, they gave us a warm-up top each and I took one look and said, 'Fuck me, that's royal not navy, that's not us at all.' I thought, 'Hold on, that's *Chelsea*! I'm not wearing that!'

We were a bit upset about it, but I quickly realised that it wouldn't make us win or lose. It's what's inside the shirt more than what is on it. It took me a while to learn this.

Roy will tell you that early on I used to be superstitious. I used to wear the same tie to every match. But as you go through your career, as you mature and get older, you work out it's nothing to do with the tie. I used to like getting to the ground early, too, but I'll tell you this, you had to get up pretty early in the morning to beat Roy to White Hart Lane. However early you were, he was there. And even if the gates were locked you'd find him in the café over the road. It's that attitude, that unbending desire for the club to be successful that made Roy critically important to Spurs.

When I worked in Japan, football there made me realise how important what I call 'shop-floor football' is to a club. What I mean is that we learned our lessons at Spurs over the course of 100 years. In Japan, they only have ten years of history. When I was cleaning boots as an apprentice, there were three trainers – one of whom was Andy Thompson who was part of the 1921 Cup Final team – and their conversation would be: 'Who was better, Burgess or Mackay?' or 'Who was our best ever captain?' All the time, this was washing over you, the history seeping into your skin.

Having people like Roy around the club, someone with so many years of dedication to the club behind him, perpetuates the very history of the club. Through people like Roy Reyland, the legend of Tottenham Hotspur lives on.

PREFACE

BY TERRY VENABLES, 2010

There have not been many books written by kit managers – in fact, I'm certain this is the first – but Roy Reyland isn't your average kit man. Like me, Roy grew up a Spurs fan and later he sat on the bench with me when Spurs won the FA Cup in 1991. For a new generation of Spurs fans, it was the greatest victory the club has seen. But after lifting the FA Cup twice for the team I supported as a boy – once as a player and again as a manager – how could I have anything less than a huge affinity for Tottenham Hotspur Football Club? Both occasions were as dramatic as they were satisfying, and for very different reasons.

I grew up in Dagenham, which is a big West Ham area, and my two best mates were dedicated Hammers fans. But in those days Spurs were much like Manchester City or Chelsea today – a powerful team with all the best players. We had Blanchflower, Mackay and some of the biggest names in the league. And as a young professional growing up, I knew that, if I were to join Spurs, I'd have a hard time getting in the team! Instead, when I left school in 1957 I signed for Chelsea as an apprentice and worked my way into the team. Eventually, I made over 200 appearances for Chelsea, narrowly missing out on winning the league.

But when you're a schoolboy, it's the not the league you dream of winning. Every game of football in the playground is an FA Cup Final! The cup was a marvellous thing in my day, and, for a young player, your greatest ambition was to play at Wembley in a cup final. For me that dream would come true in 1967, joyously, after I'd signed for Tottenham. And my opponents were, of course, my former club, Chelsea.

It was a tremendous final, the first to be contended by two London clubs and as such became known as the 'Cockney Cup Final'. For a boy from East London, the occasion was especially memorable. A hundred thousand supporters watched Spurs win 2–1, with Jimmy Robertson and Frank Saul netting the goals. By getting my hands on that trophy, it was really one in the eye for my old team.

After 115 games for Spurs, I departed for Queens Park Rangers, but I would later return to Tottenham in 1987 as manager. Again, I had a burning ambition to lift silverware, and soon after I arrived I bought a young player called Paul Gascoigne, who would become vital to that aim. I was to test out that £2m signing – and the £1.5m signing of Paul Stewart – at a friendly tournament at Wembley no less, in the summer of 1988. Among other teams, we were to face the mighty Arsenal, but it was to be a disaster.

I fielded our strongest team: Mimms, Allen, Stimson, Fenwick, Fairclough, Mabbutt, Walsh, Gascoigne, Waddle, Stewart and Samways. But Gazza was – how do I say this politely – a little out of shape. In fact, my other big signing Paul Stewart looked like he'd had a good summer, too. We were destroyed 4–0 by Arsenal, and I remember thinking that we had a lot of work to do.

But hard work is what we did. It was three years before we returned to Wembley, to face Arsenal in the FA Cup semi-final of 1991, and, as the history books will tell you, it was one hell of a match. I felt that we outplayed them, and of course Gazza was instrumental. I've not seen a free-kick like his since, and both the semi-final and the final were magical, and it made all that hard work worthwhile.

Spurs meant a great deal to me, and the manner in which I left was obviously a massive disappointment. I never wanted to leave, and I've got a massive allegiance for the Spurs fans, many of whom rallied around me and supported me when things went a bit sour. Spurs people love a fighter, and they also love a man who has a genuine dedication to the team.

When I look back at my memories with Tottenham Hotspur, there were some fantastic moments, and in almost all of them one man was present: Roy Reyland. Tottenham's loyal kit man was already part of the furniture when I arrived, and I remember Roy was always a cheery face in the dressing room. If the pitch was frozen over, the rain was coming down sideways – or worse, we'd lost – Roy would always have a smile on his face. You could see that he loved that job with his heart and soul. It was a pleasure working with Roy, and I've not had a more dedicated player on my team since.

PROLOGUE

Visitors to the Spurs kit room would always ask about the bullet holes in the walls. 'You can blame Gazza and his air rifle for those,' I used to tell them. Gazza had opened fire on his friend Jimmy 'Five Bellies', and I'd had to take cover before he came crashing through the stadium roof while hunting pigeons, all on the day before a big match. They were unbelievable times. When I first became kit man at the historic Tottenham Hotspur Football Club over three decades ago, I naively believed it would be a piece of cake: throw out 12 shirts, 12 shorts and a few towels, then go home. How wrong I was, because, with Gazza around, absolutely anything could happen.

I remember the time he walked into the dressing room wearing nothing but a pair of pants. 'Gazza,' I told him, 'it's ten minutes until kick-off, put your kit on!'

But he just smiled and told me, in his great Geordie accent, that he'd given it away to a disabled girl during the warm-up. This was typical Gazza – spontaneous, generous and lovely in every way. So I gave him another shirt, pointed at my watch and told him to hurry up. But he was still standing there, looking sheepish.

'No, Roysie, I've given her the lot,' he confessed. And so he had: shinpads, match shorts, shirts, socks, boots... everything.

I flew round that dressing room like a man possessed, hunting spare socks and shorts, desperate for our star player to make it on to the field in time. But the big problem was Gazza's boots.

'I only had one pair,' he said, and explained that he'd just signed a contract with Brooks, a boot manufacturer of the time. Knowing that he couldn't take his boots back from a little girl in a wheelchair, I grabbed a tin of black paint and quickly coloured in a pair of size-9 Puma boots for him. With three minutes left till kick-off, I was desperately trying to paint on a Brooks logo, using Tippex. Gazza made it, but only just.

In 30 years I'd done it all at White Hart Lane: I'd lovingly seeded the turf, and watched young talent blossom into professional footballers. I replaced smashed windows and repaired damaged egos, acting as an unofficial agony aunt to generations of Spurs legends. I dealt with tragedy, loss and even relegation. I celebrated two League Cup victories, worked half-a-dozen Wembley finals and won three FA Cups. I handed shirts to Glenn

Hoddle, Ricky Villa, Ossie Ardiles, Teddy Sheringham, Jürgen Klinsmann and David Ginola. And I sat on the bench next to 17 managers – from Keith Burkinshaw to George Graham and Martin Jol.

From cup final shirts with missing Holsten logos to missing centre-backs – even the case of a suspected poisoned lasagne – it all went on at Tottenham Hotspur, and, more often than not, I was right in the thick of it. And during all this madness it was my kit room that became a sanctuary for the modern-day heroes of Tottenham Hotspur, as a constellation of soccer stars would drop in to air their dirty laundry, while I laundered theirs.

I travelled the country and the world to every game at home and away, man and boy; I watched every minute of every match, becoming both a loyal member of staff, dedicated Spurs fan and an unlikely talisman to the team.

As you can see, the kit man's job was so much more than throwing out 12 shirts on a Saturday afternoon – players and managers came and went, matches were won and lost, and for 29 glorious seasons I was in charge of those famous lily-white shirts, and a whole lot more. Now, for the first time, I reveal what went on behind those dressing-room doors, and I've included the mud, the sweat and the tears. This is my story.

CHAPTER 1

'MR GREAVES, MR GREAVES!'

My first experience of Tottenham Hotspur Football Club came as an 11-year-old boy, standing outside in the pouring rain on the short road leading up to the famous gates of the stadium. It was 1967, and Bill Nicholson's Spurs had just won their third FA Cup in seven years by beating Chelsea, having already won 'the Double' in 1960/61, as well as beating Real Madrid 5–1 in the final of the European Cup Winners' Cup. They would later name that road after the manager, and, as I watched players such as Bobby Smith, Bill Brown and Jimmy Greaves drive into the ground along Bill Nicholson Way, I dreamed that one day I would be one of them. I had fallen in love with Spurs.

Welcome to my 'early years'. These are the part of most autobiographies I normally find quite boring, but in my story I hope you'll discover the roots of my early obsession with Tottenham Hotspur, and you might better understand my complete devotion to the club. I hope you'll come to realise that I love the club as much as you do, and that maybe, like me, you knew from day one that you were Spurs through and through.

I was born in North Middlesex Hospital on the borders of Tottenham and Edmonton. My parents lived on Lorenca Road, which was renowned for housing the area's toughest families. Ours wasn't a bad family, though, and soon after my birth my parents moved to Chalgrove Road, which is at the bottom of Park Lane, the road that leads to the Spurs stadium. In fact, we could see it out the window. On that road lived about 20 young lads like me, growing up in the shadow of one of Europe's most famous football stadia. I remember we used to jog up to Worcester Avenue to play football. At the time, the stadium had these big blue wooden doors, and we'd play football against them till 11pm, illuminated under the sodium streetlights. We used to have some fantastic games against those doors. We were all thick as thieves, living in each other's pockets, and, of course, we were all Spurs mad.

From the age of 11, those blue doors and late-night football became our world. We were never in trouble, and we looked after each other, and we loved Tottenham Hotspur. But I have to admit a dark secret: the first football kit I ever wore was a West Ham shirt. I think my parents liked the colour. My dad, Bill Reyland, was a great man and a decent player. He and his brothers enjoyed good amateur careers. But I knew claret and blue wasn't for me, and Spurs were my team. It was around that time I started to hang around the ground to collect autographs.

The team used to train at Cheshunt, in Hertfordshire, but if the weather was bad they would use the stadium, and even if it was bucketing down I'd go and wait for them. When I was on a school holiday, I'd always be there (and sometimes, if I'm honest, when I was meant to be at school!). But it wasn't really the autographs that enticed me to spend so much time waiting outside in the rain. It was getting close to people I associated with Spurs, those living legends. I remember seeing Eddie Clayton, Bill Brown, Bobby Smith, Alan Gilzean and Jimmy Greaves. I remember asking Cliff Jones, a player I greatly admired because he was such a tremendous header of the ball, for an autograph. I was tiny as a kid and I used to look up to him, not just with respect, but because of how much he towered over me. Looking back, he was only 5'6".

So, I'd hang around outside 'Bill Nick Way' and, as this was just after the Double years, I was meeting some of Tottenham's most famous players. They'd walk out of the little office and into the White Hart pub, and being the 1960s they'd sit in the bar having a drink! Often they'd walk down to the Bell and Hare afterwards, and I'd catch them in between and ask for an autograph. But I was always frightened to speak to them. I was in awe of them, and I used to be ever so polite. I would say, 'Excuse me, Mr Brown, could you sign this please?' My head was down and I was very meek. But they'd say, 'Of course!' Sometimes they'd even ask you questions: 'Who's your favourite player?' or 'Do you go to the matches?' I was at my happiest when I was speaking to my heroes.

Jimmy Greaves was my all-time hero. Bill Nicholson had signed him from AC Milan for £99,999, and this unusual figure was intended to relieve Greaves of the pressure of being the first £100,000 player.

Greaves enjoyed a magical career at Tottenham, playing from 1961 to 1970, scoring a club record of 266 goals in 379 matches. He finished top goal scorer in six seasons, a feat that has never been matched, and, with Spurs, Greaves won the FA Cup in 1962 and 1967, scoring against Burnley in 1962. He also won the European Cup Winners' Cup in 1963 – scoring twice in the famous 5–1 defeat of Atlético Madrid, during a fantastic game.

I'll never forget the first time I got Jimmy Greaves' autograph. I'd cut a photo out of the local newspaper and stuck it in my scrapbook. I was waiting at the ground as usual, but I didn't think any players were there. Then I suddenly saw this big car pull out of the stadium. Jimmy's car was something like a Ford Granada, and it was amazing, with a tiny boot, and a great big long bonnet: one of those cars that looked 100mph even when it was stood still – a lot like Greaves himself. I was already halfway home, under the famous clock on the

High Road, when I turned and saw Greaves in his car. And I ran! I shouldn't have done it really, but I jumped in front of his car.

'Mr Greaves, Mr Greaves!' I yelped, and the car came to a halt in front of me. I was fumbling through my scrapbook desperately trying to find my Jimmy Greaves picture, but the striker was fantastic. He said, 'Calm down, it's OK, lad.' And he signed my picture: 'All the best, Jimmy Greaves'. I'd finally got the autograph I most desired, and I ran all the way to my sister's house, which back then was on nearby Park Lane. Jean lived in a little two-up two-down, and the front door was right on the pavement, so all the crowd would bang on the windows on match day. The lady next door would open up her front room and everyone would pay pennies to park their bikes in there. It was a 20-yard stroll to the turnstile, and around that time I went to my first game, with my brother-in-law, Roger.

Roger was a massive Spurs fan and a huge instigator of my love for the club. One day he took me to see Spurs play Fulham at the Lane. I remember it because Fulham played in the opposite colours to us: dark-blue shirts, white shorts and blue socks. Even as a kid, I recall how I respected that perfect symmetry. Soon afterwards, Roger took me to see a midweek game, and it was an event that changed my life forever. I remember how cold and dark it was in Tottenham that night. We walked up the stairs and suddenly I was blinded by the floodlights. Then the team ran out, resplendent in their all-white kit... it was such a dazzling vision, an almost religious moment. I expect you've felt those same intoxicating feelings.

Spurs had finished third in the league the year before, just behind Manchester United and Nottingham Forest, and we had won the FA Cup. We had signed Mike England from Blackburn Rovers and Terry Venables from Chelsea, and we would have won the Double again had Spurs not thrown their chances away in October and November in a series of needless home defeats.

My first season watching Spurs was, in comparison, a disappointing season. However, it was a year all Spurs fans will remember for a very special goal – scored by goalkeeper Pat Jennings in the Charity Shield. In a mixed season, Spurs destroyed West Ham 5–1, Burnley 5–0 and Southampton 6–1 in April, yet Greaves scored only 23 goals from 39 appearances, and Spurs finished just seventh in the First Division.

I used to love going to White Hart Lane more than anything in the world. I remember standing on a stool and getting completely carried away by the swell of the crowd. Sometimes, when something happened on the pitch, the crowd would suddenly lift me off my feet and we would all sway forward and sway back, and I was carried around on a wave of Spurs supporters. Somehow, I'd always end up back at the same place, and my feet would land right back on the stool!

I'd always try to get in front of a barrier, because if there was a surge you'd be protected. At one big game, the ground was packed, and they lifted a lot of us kids in front of the wall to watch the game from the side of the pitch. I could smell the rich aroma of the turf. It all seemed so close, and the dream seemed so achievable.

My sister bought me my first Spurs kit when I was 12, but by then I was playing for the school team and, like all young boys, I secretly harboured a dream of playing in that kit for real. I wanted to play for Tottenham Hotspur, and I wanted to be Jimmy Greaves. All those nights playing up against the wall in the street started to pay off, and I was playing regularly for Somerset School in Crayton Road, right opposite Bill Nicholson's house. We were a phenomenal school team, and I don't remember losing once. Many of the team were picked to play for Tottenham Boys, Middlesex Boys or London Boys, depending on how good they were. And I was delighted, aged 13, to be invited to train with Tottenham Boys at a local school called Rowland Hill every Saturday morning.

The coach, Dicky Moss, later became goalkeeping coach for the Spurs Schoolboys. He seemed about 150 years old to me, with long General Custer hair, and a lisp... he was such a character. For a brief time it looked like I might make it as a professional: I was left-footed, strong on the ball and an asset to any team. To play for Tottenham Boys was a dream come true, though I remember I was disappointed we never had the cockerel on our shirts. Instead, Tottenham Boys played in blank white shirts, but, like any local boy, I dreamed of pulling on that famous shirt, and scoring for Spurs.

I did my best to impress the Spurs scouts who flocked down to watch us. During my first game for Tottenham Boys, I was on the left wing and a boy called Peter Tunget crossed the ball and I leapt up to header it, and the ball flew just over the bar. The balls in those days were heavy and stitched together with lace, and this one nicked my left eye. It was my first touch for Tottenham Boys, and it had ripped open my eye. I finished the game with a permanent memento of the game – I'd played for Tottenham Boys and I had the scar to prove it.

Eventually, I got invited to train on Tuesdays with the real Tottenham Hotspur, and my dream looked like it might come true. The Spurs' youth team trained on a hard ball court, and all the Spurs coaches were there. Just the fact that you were associated with Tottenham Hotspur was amazing and I walked with a skip in my step during those beautiful days. I showed great promise, and a few people might tell you I was destined for a professional career. Alas, the months progressed and so did the other boys, but it was becoming clear I was not meant to become a six-footer and, tragically, because of my size, I was released.

Of course, I was heartbroken. Roger used to stand me up at the Park Lane end every weekend, and every game I saw I'd dream of pulling on that shirt. The only player that made pro level from Tottenham Boys was Stevie Phillips. He lived on Crayton Road, near Bill Nicholson. 'Eggy' Phillips, we called him, although I can't remember why. Later he made his debut for Birmingham City, against Spurs, and Pat Jennings was in goal. It was the only time I've ever wanted Spurs to get beaten, because I'd played in the same team as Phillips and I was just willing him to score.

Those were 'standing' days at White Hart Lane, and the atmosphere was electric. I used to stand behind the Park Lane goal and the visiting fans used to stand among us, but there was rarely any trouble. I remember the old programmes, with the team set out in formation order on the back. Roger, ever the entrepreneur, would cut them all out, take the tiny pieces of paper and shake them up in his hand and sell them to blokes in the crowd. You'd pick one for a penny and the first goal scorer would win the pot. It was absolutely brilliant, and, although it was for a tiny amount of money, it would really increase the tension, as you willed on the left back to score an unlikely opening goal to win you the pot.

Spurs were a great team to watch in those days and very much a passing team. The game was of course slower, and the pitch probably wasn't the best either, but Cliff Jones was so fast. Those were the days of Beal, Brown, Gilzean and Greaves, and I was quickly becoming a huge Spurs fan, but primarily a football fan.

Then Roger bought a television and we started watching the televised matches. During cup finals, I'd write the names of the teams on paper and stick them on to the TV set. As they scored, I'd put the scores up on the telly. It took years for the BBC to make my job as scorekeeper redundant, by putting the scores up on the screen themselves.

I was equally obsessed with my autograph book: you could read every single autograph, as the handwriting in those days was good and old-fashioned. Those albums were outstanding; I used to buy magazines and newspapers and pictures from the Spurs shop, and I would stick them in those books, all in perfect order, and all of them signed. I was fanatical about the players being in order and everything laid out 'just so'.

Around this time, Roger and I got into Subbuteo. I quickly became obsessed with it, and soon I had 54 teams. My first was Motherwell, because I was taken by their red and yellow stripes. I had the floodlights, the stadium, the crowd, the works – Roger and my sister really spoiled me. I had league tables, held FA Cup competitions and had books and books of scores from the myriad games that Roger and I would play against each other. It was a miracle my sister didn't ask for a divorce, the amount of time Roger spent with me and not her! It was safe to say they looked after me like a son.

I wish I still had those Subbuteo results books today.

On a Sunday, Roger and my sister would come to my mum's house for lunch, and afterwards we would disappear upstairs to play Subbuteo, from seven o'clock to eleven o'clock at night. Everything was regimented and perfectly laid out, including my growing autograph collection. I must have had eight albums in all, all fully signed: amounting to a whole childhood's work. But one day, when I turned 16, I gave them away to the lad next door. He was only ten, and we used to play head tennis over the fence. He said one day, 'I really like Spurs, they're my team.' So I went back in the house, picked up the books and handed them over the fence. The lot. It was the end of a chapter for me, and reluctantly, with my football dreams over, I went to work with my dad at the firm he worked for, Beautility Furniture.

Dad had been working there 25 years when suddenly he fell ill. And very sadly, he passed away soon afterwards. I carried on working for the firm, but it was such a vast company that even months after he'd passed I'd see someone I hadn't seen for a few months and he'd say, 'Sorry to hear about your dad.' I couldn't handle it, and I left. I just couldn't accept that I'd lost my dad at such an early age.

I was playing for Ware and Hertford, good semi-professional teams, and my dad missed all that. I remember he saw me play once in my early years, when I got picked to play for the league against the Maccabi League for Jewish boys. But Dad passed away just before I was 18, and, although I don't drink, I often regret that I never got the chance to have a beer with my old man. And one of my biggest regrets is that I never went to Spurs with my dad.

Nevertheless, I still kept playing football, and I went back and played in the Edmonton Sunday league, for Park Royal, and then the best team in the league, called Crown. But the loss of my dad had left a huge hole in my life, and I was fortunate that my brother-in-law Roger spent so much time with me, and always took me to the games. Although I missed my dad awfully, I really threw myself into supporting Spurs. And it was a fine time to be supporting the boys in white. In 1972, we played in the first ever UEFA Cup football tournament and progressed to the final where we met Wolverhampton Wanderers in a two-legged contest. We were victorious, winning the tie 3–2 on aggregate, after a 2–1 victory away from home, in which Martin Chivers scored a remarkable late winner from 25 yards. Then we drew 1–1 in the second leg at White Hart Lane, eventually winning the competition and becoming European champions. It was a remarkable time to be a Spurs fan living in Tottenham.

Football became my life, and Spurs my everything, as I tried to distract myself from the loss of my father. But times were hard for a single-parent family in the 1970s, and I realised I had to quickly become a man. I started work as a window cleaner, but I was desperate to find a job that would excite me as much as football, that might give me the same buzz as Spurs and Subbuteo. It was then that my mum got a job as a cleaner for Tottenham Hotspur Football Club, and one night she came home with the news that there was a job available at White Hart Lane, on the ground staff. I thought, 'Why not?'

CHAPTER 2

THE GOING GETS TURF

I signed for Tottenham Hotspur as a 22-year-old in 1978, only not as a left-winger as originally intended, but as a member of the ground staff. Which was lucky, because, if they had given me a medical, I would have failed, having picked up a knee injury playing amateur football. And in a brief glimpse into the fantastic treatment I was to receive from the club, Mike Varney, the physio, said he'd take a look at my knee, which was causing me much trouble. I hadn't been at the club long, so I was startled at the personal treatment I was receiving.

They told me I'd need a small operation and that the official Spurs surgeon, a talented man called Pat England, would perform it. It all sounded straightforward but, after the operation in the nearby Queen Anne Hospital, I woke up to discover that I had a plaster cast from groin to toe, which was devastating and very frightening.

'When Mr England operated,' the doctor told me, 'it turned out you'd torn your anterior ligament.' This was a disaster! He went on, 'We've taken some ligament out of your knee, we've tightened up the ligaments and we've pinned them.'

I said, 'Hang on, I need to get a grip of what is happening here. How long before I can play again?'

I'll never forget his exact words: 'Let's make sure you can walk again, first.'

Now, when Mr England came back, I tearfully recounted what the doctor had told me. 'Roy, you *will* walk and you *will* play again, don't worry,' he said. 'Nine months, and you'll be playing again.'

To a bystander, you'd think the Spurs surgeon was talking to a centre forward with his career on the line! But that's how they made me feel. The club completely rehabilitated me, as if I *was* a player. I used to go to treatment in the morning and do my ground-staff duty in the afternoon. Nine months and one day after the op, I was invited to play in a staff game, and once again I was kicking a ball, wearing lily-white and blue. I was back where I belonged, on the pitch, playing for Tottenham... in some capacity. You see, when you've got Tottenham Hotspur in your blood, it never leaves you. I suppose that's why they sing on the terraces, 'I'm Tottenham Till I Die.' I knew then that I'd be at the club for as long as I could.

Mick Stockwell, the man who interviewed me for the

position, was in charge of telling me all about life at the club. When I asked him, 'What does the job consist of?' he just smiled and said, 'Everything'. He went on, 'One day you'll be a plumber, another day an electrician, a glazer, a groundsman, anything and everything.'

And he was right. For four years, I did just about every job in that stadium.

After every Saturday game, we used to come in on the Monday and sweep the stadium. We used to sweep every row, and then sweep the terracing, then everything else. Can you believe it took us three days to sweep the entire White Hart Lane stadium, and there were ten of us at it? You swept all the stands, seats, the concourses, underneath the enclosure and the car parks. And if there was a midweek game, they'd employ part-timers to come in and get it all crashed out in time for Saturday. Sweeping White Hart Lane was like painting the Forth Bridge – as soon as it was finished, it needed doing again!

We used to do all the cleaning too, including the toilets, the offices and the dressing rooms. I swear I've done more sweeping at White Hart Lane than Ledley King! But as an introduction to working at Spurs, it was invaluable. I got to know my way round that ground like it was the back of my hand. I've fixed the plumbing in the toilets, replaced light bulbs in the boardrooms, and, rather touchingly, it was one of my jobs to paint those big blue doors on the Worcester Avenue end of the stadium. The very same doors I'd spent my childhood pelting with footballs.

One of the worst jobs I ever did at the Lane was replacing the windows at the Worcester Avenue end. We had to take away the glass and replace it with Perspex, because local kids kept putting them through with their footballs. I've never been so cold, because it was midwinter, and the second you took the glass out, the biting cold wind howled through. But you know, doing the shitty jobs was all made worthwhile because you were doing it for Tottenham Hotspur. You got out what you put in, and Tottenham was one of the most exciting clubs to be with during this period in our history.

We'd just been promoted after a brief sojourn in Division 2, where we'd been relegated for the first time since 1950. From the very start of the 1976/77 season, Spurs had been in trouble, and Keith Burkinshaw, in his maiden season as manager at White Hart Lane, struggled to bring home the results. Martin Chivers had left to play in Switzerland, and John Duncan – Spurs' top scorer for the previous two seasons – spent the season on the treatment table, leaving our forward line as effective as that proverbial chocolate teapot. The defence wasn't much better, and, despite the signing of John Gorman, injuries rocked the team, with even the reliable goalkeeper Pat Jennings being ruled out.

If we were to fail to impress the White Hart Lane faithful in the league, worse was to come in the cup. We crashed out to Second Division Cardiff City in the FA Cup and, worse, to Third Division Wrexham in the League Cup. Spurs finished rock bottom in the First

Division, and were promptly relegated, much to the dismay of the fans, many of whom took it for granted that Tottenham Hotspur would forever be a First Division outfit. But the board kept their faith in Burkinshaw, who did everything he could to send Spurs straight back to where they belonged.

As Spurs fans spent the summer of 1978 watching the World Cup, held in Argentina, they contemplated life back in the First Division. Like them, I had watched Ossie Ardiles win the World Cup on television that summer, with no idea that he would be coming to play for Spurs. I was bursting with excitement when rumour suggested that Ossie and Ricky Villa would come to Spurs. Ricky was a bit-part player in that World Cup, and Keith Burkinshaw had tried initially to sign just him, but somehow we compromised and a deal was struck that included Ossie too. It turned out to be a dream partnership, and a bargain to boot. I had just started at Tottenham myself, and I remember when they first turned up to training, these two foreign lads with World Cup winners' medals – it was frankly unbelievable. Just awesome. Keith had brought, essentially, the first International stars to the First Division. The team was never going to be the same again.

Looking back at Spurs at the time, prior to those boys arriving, we already had Steve Perryman, Steve Archibald, Glenn Hoddle and Tony Galvin. This was becoming some team. As an onlooker, it was interesting to see the two Argentineans fitting into London life and the fast pace of what was then the First Division. Ossie settled in more quickly than Ricky. He was more confident and he adapted to the game quicker. Then Ricky... well, Ricky just evolved. He would come into his own. Ossie picked the game up by the scruff of the neck and just played, but Ricky added another dimension. I used to watch them train whenever I could, and I have to admit I've never seen skill like it, the Argentines fitting in well with the English stars we had, like Glenn Hoddle.

Hoddle was a magnificent player, and a great man. I lived near Glenn in Harlow, and I used to have a drink with him occasionally, as I used to play for his uncle Dave's Sunday team. Glenn and Chrissie Waddle used to watch us play sometimes, and Glenn even managed the side for a while! It was quite the role reversal, them watching one of the ground staff play.

Being able to watch the Spurs matches for free was of course a major perk of being on the ground staff. Instead of standing up behind the Park Lane end with my brother-in-law Roger, I sat with the rest of the staff in a little pen next to the tunnel, with benches specially reserved for us to enjoy the game. Ask anyone who's ever sat on the bench and they will tell you, it is a pretty crap view. It's just a mess of legs, running around. But you get used to it, and today watching football from any other angle seems alien. If I go and watch a game at the Lane now and I sit upstairs, it doesn't look very quick at all. You see all this space that you don't appreciate from

18

the touchline, because at grass-roots level everything looks so fast.

And with Ardiles, Villa and Hoddle we became a very quick team, the fast Argentines setting an impossible pacemaker for the rest of the league. Together they made the most exciting midfield in the country, although the rest of the team needed a little while to bed in. We only finished in mid-table in the 1978/88 season, and made just the last eight of the FA Cup. But the team began to grow, and in May 1980 Spurs signed Steve Archibald from Aberdeen and later Garth Crooks from Stoke City. Like the Argentines they were both quick, and perfect accessories to the sublime skills of Glenn Hoddle. And by 1980 we had a formidable defence, too. We had an old-fashioned bruiser of a player, Paul Miller, at centre half, and he and Graham Roberts, who was called up to the first team in 1980, were like rocks. They would bash people for free, given the chance. Graham came from non-league football, and he later captained the team and even played for England. You don't hear many stories like that any more – a player climbing that ladder to such dizzying heights.

I spent that season high up a ladder, too. I think I must have painted nearly every surface of that stadium. All the crash barriers were painted silver, while in the old enclosure we had blue panelling, and I really enjoyed painting them. I used to concrete the steps, too, as they broke away under the force of 40,000 fans trampling over them week in and week out. And I decorated everywhere, from the toilets to the boardroom. My boss then, Micky Stockwell, was a great character and a fabulous man. He was a dead ringer for Sid James. Micky, the maintenance foreman, knew every stopcock, every nail or screw in that entire stadium. We had a painter called Freddy Gold, who was also a great character. When I first started, we sat in this tiny room before work and I used to see him with a massive wad of money, and I'd think, 'He must be rich!' That is, until much later I noticed that he used to wrap his banknotes round an old toilet roll!

Then there was Bill Fox; he was a painter too, and another likely lad. Everyone had a bit of banter, and everyone mucked in – they were great times. I worked with 'fishy' Bill, although I can't print why we called him that, and Harry Crossley, a man who with his wife used to put up the young players at their home. Harry looked after Graeme Souness, when he ran back to Scotland homesick, but later returned. Harry always kept in touch with Graeme, and they are still really very close. There were probably five or six of us on the ground staff, and, although the work was tough, the thing was that I didn't care what I did, so long as it was for Spurs. You see, when you join the team, it becomes personal.

In those days, we also used to do the pitch as well. Bill Nicholson was a consultant in that era, and, although Keith Burkinshaw was now manager, Bill had a big say in the pitch. I remember seeding the six-yard box myself, by hand, using a six-inch plank of wood. You'd seed the length of the plank, move it, and start again. It was painstaking. But the thing with Bill was that he never asked you to do anything or told you what to do: he was out there with you, so I spent one happy summer's day with Bill Nicholson, hand-seeding the pitch. It is a fond memory.

'Bill Nick' was 'the man' when I started at Spurs. I had only been at the club a few weeks before I met Bill properly and, when he came over, I felt very nervous and excited. Bill grasped my hand with his, and said, 'Welcome to the club, son. This is a great club, a family club, and you'll get looked after here.' I had quite an affinity for Bill.

Over the years we would grow closer, and in the mid-Eighties I remember taking my two dogs into the ground on my day off to pick something up. I took them in to meet Bill, and he made such a fuss of them. Bill and his wife, Darkie, used to send me a Christmas card, but from that year on, it was always 'To Roy and family and dogs'. Bill was a lovely, lovely man. He was fantastic to work with and a fascinating man-manager. If you ever talk to people like Steve Perryman, and many of the staff who worked with him, they will say he was authoritative, but he never ranted or raved. His motivational skills were second to none. You'd be painting a panel and he'd make it his business to come and talk to you, and it made us love him.

But back to the late Seventies, when I was really finding my feet at the club. Still a young man in my early twenties, I would enjoy messing around with the apprentices and the other young lads on the staff. The groundsman, Colin White, who started at the same time as me, was a very funny man and a typical Southampton lad with an endearing south coast accent. We struck up a great relationship, and were like two toe rags at Spurs. If there was something to get up to, we'd be in the thick of it, and along with Andy Church, the training groundskeeper, we were like the three amigos. Myself, Colin and Andy would become famous for our pranks with the youth players, and this would really make our name around the club.

Once, Colin and I were over in the car park, kicking lumps of polystyrene into skips. We were just passing the time really, having a bit of fun. We saw Tony Parks, Ian Culverhouse and their gang of apprentices strolling over, and we hatched a plan. The liquid used to whiten the lines was like a chalk white paint, so we got a real heavy, stippled brick and dipped it in the pot, and I swear you wouldn't tell the difference between that rock-hard brick and the innocent lumps of polystyrene!

Well, Tony being Tony, came over all cocky and said, 'I'll show you why I'm going to be a pro and you two will just be ground staff forever!' (He was very cocky in those days.) And with that, he took an almighty kick at the 'brick' and it didn't move an inch. The language was unbelievable! Talk about turning the air blue. We all ran for it, when suddenly, Tony threw a shovel, and it flew over our heads and stuck straight in the wall, and the handle snapped off! If it had hit either of us in the neck, we'd have been killed instantly. But, oh, how we laughed!

We used to get up to all sorts of mischief in those days. When builders were pulling down the old stand, we would nick their dumper trucks and race them up and down the East Stand concourse, where today you buy your hotdogs and beers. The old East Stand used to have metal pillars but you could walk the whole length, and we would have terrific races between ground staff and players in those dumpsters. We could have killed ourselves, but it was great fun. Competition was fierce between staff and apprentices, and there was an old pool table in the West Stand where we held epic matches. It was the shabbiest old table you could imagine, with a huge rip on the surface, a hell of a roll, and no tips on the cues.

One day Colin and I were playing Mark Falco and Micky Hazard, who were trainees at the time, and it was a tense finale. Falco was on the black, to win, and missed the winning shot, leaving the black ball waiting agonisingly over the pocket. Now, these games weren't just competitive – professional footballers don't have it in them to treat any competitions as less than life or death – and I was very nervous as Colin passed me the cue. He whispered to me, 'Hit the ball slowly... then run!'

I hit it so slowly, sending the cue ball trundling towards the black, and we both turned and ran! I ran all the way down the concourse of the West Stand, and you could hear these snooker balls bouncing along the floor; they were launching the whole lot after us!

Tommy Heffernan used to head snooker balls for money. The Irish centre half would bet cash that he could head a snooker ball, and would make extra cash on the side. Little things, when you look back, were actually quite dangerous, but often just as funny. One day, Colin was cutting the grass, sat on the big lawnmower. A few apprentices and me hatched a plan to grab him off the mower, for a laugh. Then we stripped him completely naked! Every piece of clothing he had on was divided up and raised up the flagpoles on opposite sides of the ground! Shoes, pants, the lot.

Colin being Colin, he took the joke, got straight back on the mower and, with it being a lovely sunny afternoon, carried on cutting the grass, as naked as the day he was born. But that's not the end of the story. In those days, the directors' box was sealed off by metal shutters that could only be opened from the inside. And with the sun coming out, the directors decided to come out for much-needed fresh air. What they all saw was the sight of Colin, sat completely naked on the mower, bold as brass, mowing the grass!

Another time, soon after we signed Steve Archibald, the striker and his glamorous wife were standing in the goalmouth, having photographs taken by the press. It was a great shot, but it was somewhat ruined when Colin White 'accidentally' turned the sprinkler on behind the goal, soaking the pair of them. Archie was not best pleased, to say the least!

They were fun times, and our escapades brought us all

together as a team. I enjoyed mucking in with the apprentices, and many of them went on to become first-team stars. I was forging relationships with players that were about to become big names, and I was about to get a promotion myself...

CHAPTER 3
LEARNING THE ROPES

The Spurs kit man at the time was called Johnny Wallis, and he was the most miserable and cantankerous old man you could wish to meet. I remember the first time I ever walked into the kit room – which was a corner room tucked away in the car park – Johnny and Cecil Poynton, the physio, were wearing long white coats as they cleaned the boots and bleached the shirts. They looked like Doctor Death and his mate! Players used to have to beg Johnny for a sock, yet when you got to know him he had a remarkable sense of humour, and what's more he had earned the utmost respect from players and staff alike. And for that reason, I liked him. So, when Spurs manager Keith Burkinshaw pulled me aside one afternoon and asked me if I'd like to help out Johnny, I said, 'Sure.'

Johnny Wallis had been a player in the war years, and

had shrapnel in his calf. So he retired and became the old-fashioned trainer, or 'sponge man'. Later he took over as kit man, doing the job for 30 years and becoming part of the furniture at White Hart Lane. But at the time I had no idea that I would later become his successor and that, between us, just two men would have looked after those famous white shirts for nearly 60 years.

Becoming Johnny's understudy quickly seemed like hard work. But the boss had told me to help him out, so I knew I had to get stuck in. Johnny was 5'5" with a bald head and glasses and was a very clinical man. Now, I thought *I* had OCD with my autograph books and obsessive Subbuteo matches, but Johnny was absolutely meticulous and I think I caught the worst, or best, of it from him.

But there was more to come. 'It's all getting a bit much for him,' Keith told me one afternoon, and, to be fair, Johnny must have been in his sixties.

With Spurs growing as a club, there were suddenly more teams, more away kits and bigger squads. Tottenham Hotspur was becoming a big operation. So on a Monday, after the weekend's games, I'd help Johnny sort all the boots and dirty kit. I soon got into the swing of things and, on a Friday, I'd learn to pack the kit for the reserve team's game. Johnny showed me how we dealt with ordering kit from the manufacturer, which was then made by Le Coq Sportif.

This was the centenary year, and the shirt had a huge crest, with two-tone white stripes. It was beautiful. The shorts were silky, and I remember how Glenn used to wear them very short, while the leisurewear was nothing short of enviable. Johnny introduced me to the system, and told me in no uncertain terms what he expected of me. And as well as the ropes, I also learned that, if I could achieve just half the respect and admiration of Johnny Wallis, I'd be doing well. I joyously embedded myself in the world of football strips, lists and ordering systems.

In those days, the kit man used to be in control of the youth players, and that meant supervising them cleaning toilets and scrubbing boots. It was harder back then. You used to have a 'top man' – the lead youth player – who looked after the rest. One such player was loveable goalkeeper Tony Parks, subject of my earlier prank with the 'polystyrene' brick. He'd report to Johnny and say, 'The away team dressing room's spotless, home team and referees rooms are sparkling,' and Johnny would say, 'Are you sure, Tony?' Sometimes you'd let them go home for the day, other times you'd go and check or make them do it again, even if it was right – you know, just to see how they react to a bit of discipline.

One particular time, Tony went up to Johnny and said, 'I'm done, it's all clean.'

Tony had on a beautiful white shirt, and was clearly ready to go home after a hard day's training and cleaning. Johnny ran his finger across the top of the dressing-room door, looked at his finger and ran it right down the middle of Tony's shirt, leaving a horrendous black line of grease. 'Do it again,' he sighed. And Tony simply turned on his heels and started cleaning the dressing room all over again, without muttering a word of complaint. Was Johnny too tough, or was it character building? Well, soon afterwards Tony Parks became Spurs' hero against Anderlecht in the 1984 UEFA Cup Final, saving two penalties to win us the trophy. He was just 21.

I too, was doing a lot of growing up. My job had changed from being a novelty to suddenly being a reality. I had a job to do now. Two in fact, because I did a season combining my ground-staff duties and the reserve-team kit duties. I recall Bill Nick saying to me, 'You'll be all right here, you might not always see eye-to-eye with Johnny, but look, learn and listen.' I soon started as a full-time assistant kit man and started travelling to the reserve games. In those days, when the first team were away, the reserves played at White Hart Lane. I don't know what havoc that caused with the pitch, but you'd get anything up to 3,000 supporters along, and, when we played Arsenal, you could expect up to 10,000 fans there. It was electric.

Doug Livermore, the famous Scouse star, was in charge of the reserve team when I became kit man. He'd played for Liverpool, and against Spurs for Norwich in the League Cup Final. Spurs beat them 2–1. Doug came to Spurs as a coach and he was brilliant. I always thought he was Mr Nice Guy – and he was – but one day I saw him really lose his rag and I quickly learned that you shouldn't judge someone too soon. I remember thinking, 'I never want to cross Doug.'

Once, the reserves played Millwall away at the Old Den, and it was a great game, with the ball flying from end to end and goals aplenty. Spurs were on the attack when suddenly a fella tapped me on the shoulder in the dugout, and said, 'I want to play for Spurs.'

Now, you'd occasionally get some idiot who thinks you can just ask for a game, but, when I turned round, I saw the biggest man mountain I had ever seen! He was about six-foot-six tall and wide, one of the scariest Millwall thugs! And he wanted to play for Spurs! I tapped Dougie, because I wasn't getting involved in this one. I said, 'Doug, there's a fella here who wants to speak to you.'

He replied, 'Yeah, yeah, Roy, I'm busy.'

But the bloke was still pestering me, so I said, 'Doug, he really wants to play for Spurs.'

Doug turned to me, and he was about to tell this bloke to sling his hook, when he too suddenly clocked the size of him, and he said quickly, and ever-so politely, 'Leave your name and address with me, son...' It was brilliant.

The reserve team was pretty hot at the time, with players like Ian Crook, Tony Parks, Ian Culverhouse, Peter Southey and Mark Bowen all making appearances. Even big players like Ray Clemence and Chrissie Waddle would play in the reserves when they were coming back from injury, so often the team was as star-studded as the first team! It was an early taste of working with some of Tottenham's biggest names, like David Howells who had a spell in the team. The reserve team league was called the Combination and we finished top a couple of times, and won the Combination Cup. Occasionally, you'd have one of the under-18 boys in the team, playing alongside the likes of Chrissie Waddle. If you ask me, it was fantastic for the younger players and I began to really enjoy being involved in the reserves.

The reserves games were always so competitive. It was full-on, because every player was either fighting to prove their worth or their fitness. Goalkeeper Tony Parks really stood out. He always had such wit and character – he was a confident boy and he played that way, even as a teenager. Micky Hazard used to shine in that reserve team, and I personally think that Micky was unlucky to be in the same era as Glenn Hoddle, for his ability on the ball was amazing. But getting in that team ahead of a player like Hoddle was beyond him, or anyone else for that matter.

So why didn't players like Glenn or Stevie Perryman ever leave? As Bill Nicholson had told me, we played good football, there was a good atmosphere and we were a family club. Who would want to leave? Stevie sacrificed his England career for Spurs, he'll happily admit. He just loved his Spurs. I remember he had what he called his 'fat ankle'. It was permanently swollen, because he'd refuse to miss a game. Stevie would be last out of the dressing room because he'd ice his fat ankle, then have it strapped – he never liked to miss a game. If you look at photos of him playing, look at his ankles and I'll guarantee one will be swollen. He just played on it because, like everyone else, he wanted to be on the team.

I'd caught the same bug, and, from when I first started work with my dad at Beautility furniture to my last day at Spurs, I never had a day off sick. I've gone to work in terrible states and even been sent home, but I have always attended. It stems from my dad, who was a stickler for not being tardy. He told me as a kid, 'You've always got to go in.' So, even if I turned up and vomited in the dressing room, at least I tried. And when I was at Tottenham, I hated missing a day's work, because it was more than just a job.

It was unlike any other job I've ever done. Some of my mates became painters, printers and couriers, but my job caused a stir when I told people. They'd ask, 'What's it like?' I'd just answer, 'It's hard work.' Because I couldn't explain it any other way. I felt like a crucial member of that team. The job was gruelling, more so than you could ever imagine. But I loved it.

Every morning Johnny and I used to leave the main stadium at 8.50am; I had the job of driving the mini-bus, with wicker skips full of training kit stacked on the roof rack. One of the apprentices would get on top and we'd throw it up. Then I'd drive them from White Hart Lane to Cheshunt, up the A10, with the apprentices in the back. Imagine the banter! We'd get there about 9.30, drag all the stuff off the top, and me and the boys would lay out the dressing rooms for the first team, the reserves and the Academy. Then, Johnny and me would drive the van back to the Lane, where the laundry ladies would have washed the previous day's kit. For years, there was always a wash on, as we had one set of kit in the wash, one on the players' backs and one spare. Then we'd start preparing the match kit for the Under 17s, Under 18s and the reserves' weekend games. You're talking thousands of items of kit, and it was quite the operation. Then we'd be back to the training ground to pick up the dirty stuff.

The laundry ladies were unbelievable. One of them, Sylvie, was there in 1978 when I joined and she must have done 20 years' service before leaving. She was less of a laundry lady, more a magician, such was her ability to make stains disappear from those white shirts. Sometimes the kit was horrific – so rank you wouldn't touch it. But Sylvie just sorted it, as if on autopilot. Like me, she was a perfectionist, and nothing was too much trouble. She had two massive industrial machines, one dryer and one spin dryer at White Hart Lane, and she'd get there as early as Johnny and me, keen as mustard.

I'd started to really admire Johnny Wallis, because he was a no-nonsense man who made the job look easy. Johnny never used to have any lists, but, although he never had names or squad numbers to deal with, and you could argue that was easier, he did it all off the top of his head and never forgot a thing. Myself, I needed a checklist. I had 60 printed off in the office and I would religiously check the list as I worked. Johnny also had this knack of being abrupt, and strong, and sometimes even quite offensive to the apprentices. He used to tell me, 'Test them. See how they react to criticism.' But I was only 26 and I was nervous about doing that, at first.

Johnny was a stickler for timing and getting things done. I was always lenient to the apprentices and I'd wait in the car park for them to arrive if they were late, but he wouldn't have that. One day Johnny was pulling out of Bill Nick Way, and when he got to the end of the road we saw some apprentices who'd just got off the train, running towards us. Of course, they were late, and they were 30 yards away. But Johnny sped off, leaving them there, stranded. As he put his foot down, I asked him why he didn't wait. 'What time did they go home yesterday?' he asked.

'Half-four,' I said.

'Well,' Johnny said sternly, 'they've had from half-four to half-eight this morning to get here and they're late. Unlucky.'

And those boys were never late again.

Sometimes, Johnny was just as harsh to me, too. He'd snarl, 'Do that' and 'Do this' and I'd say, 'Slow down!' But we soon became close. He'd tell me trade secrets, like how to keep boots soft. Johnny used to wipe them off right after the game with a damp cloth – he'd never hang them in direct heat – and then he'd place them in a naturally heated room so the leather didn't shrink. After that, with a bit of black boot polish and dubbing, they'd be perfect, and the players would be happy.

And when the players were happy, the results came in. Spurs were going great guns, and we got to the 1981 FA Cup Final against Manchester City, one of the most exciting finals in football history. The game was played over two legs and what people tend to erase from history was that Ricky Villa played a real stinker in the first game. When I used to watch him train, I always noticed how he was so laidback. He had this great ability of drifting past players, and, boy, could he play the ball. But he could also drift in and out of games, and would often either have a fantastic game or a poor game. This was one of his poorer games.

Some spectators think that, on the wages they earn, players should play great every game, but anyone who has played to any decent level knows that's just not possible. If you don't have at least seven players firing on all cylinders, you've got a problem. I remember after that first final, which we drew, Ricky was trudging off with that gold chain swinging around his neck. I really felt for him, as it was the Argentine lads' first big moment in England, and the FA Cup had such prestige in those days.

During the build-up to the next game, everyone was thinking: 'Are they going to drop him?' But Keith had said to Ricky, 'You're playing, no matter what happens.' And that really made the difference to Ricky.

In the second final, I was sitting behind the goal and I saw Ricky as he started on that mazy run. I was thinking, 'Good one, Ricky, now pass it.' Then, 'Oh, well done. Now pass it.' Then... 'OK, you've beaten two, please pass it!' He went to shoot, but didn't, then checked inside once again. Now, next time you watch the goal, try to watch Garth Crooks instead of Ricky, because he's swinging his right foot, kicking every ball with him, as if he was urging him to hit it! It's hilarious! Of course, the rest is history.

The reception was in the Chanticleer banqueting rooms, next door to White Hart Lane. It was a fantastic evening. We came out at six the next morning and went straight to the café for breakfast. I don't normally drink, but I drank that night and I couldn't walk! What great memories. To be a part of a successful club was intoxicating in many ways.

Back at work, Johnny had started to give me hints, like dropping little trade secrets, not just about keeping shirts whiter than white, but how to keep players happy. It was such a big arena and a big stage on which to make a major cock-up. Everyone's human, but sometimes something would go wrong that no one could help. Johnny told me that, before one away match, the traffic was so bad that he had the players get dressed on the coach. He stopped the bus, got the skips out from underneath, and the lads got stripped off on board. Johnny was always calm under pressure. And as I suspected, he was starting to groom me for the big job.

I became closer to the players, making sure they had everything they needed, and becoming a bit of a 'go-to' guy if they needed anything special. I remember one particular afternoon – 3 April 1982 – when we played Leicester in the FA Cup semi-final. We won, and tremendously; Spurs were on their way to Wembley once again. But one member of the squad was not smiling as widely as the rest of the players: Ossie Ardiles had a concerned look on his face. The day before the match, Ossie's home nation, Argentina, had invaded the British-owned Falkland Islands, starting what would escalate into the Falklands War. While British and Argentine relationships were flourishing at Tottenham Hotspur, international relationships were strained, and Ossie confessed to me that he was worried about his future.

'It is incredibly sad how these two countries I love could be at war against each other,' he told me. 'This is terrible.'

Later, Mr Burkinshaw tried to reassure Ossie, telling him, 'Don't worry, people will only think about football. They all love you,' and so on.

But, worried about what might happen if the war escalated, Ossie reluctantly took a one-year loan to French side Paris Saint-Germain. And in order to make his journey to the French capital easier on the stressed player, Keith Burkinshaw asked me if I'd like to help Ossie move house. Of course I was flattered, but I was also excited about helping one of my favourite players.

I took a hired van to Broxbourne, Hertfordshire, where Ossie lived, and picked up all of his belongings. He didn't have any furniture, it was more personal belongings, but there was enough of it. Ossie flew to Paris, and I booked the ferry and drove down to Dover, then across France to Paris. I was to stay for two nights in the Hotel Concorde Lafayette, a posh hotel right near the Champs-Elysées. It was mind-blowing: the hotel was, and still is, a Parisian landmark and it was truly an amazing experience. I drove right around the Arc de Triomphe and it was like wacky races. I'd never driven abroad before and I was terrified by the French driving! Ossie had given me some cash to tide me over for the journey, for petrol and suchlike, but, as soon as I had finished my first coffee in Hotel Concorde Lafayette, I realised I was in trouble. '*How* much?!' I asked the waiter incredulously. '*That* much, for a coffee?'

When Ossie arrived at the hotel the next morning to take delivery of his belongings, he asked me how I liked the hotel. 'It's great, Ossie,' I said, 'but I've run out of money already!'

Ossie paid the bill and he handed me a wad of francs, and smiled. 'Here you go, Roysie, for your food and whatever else.' It was a generous amount.

We drove together to Ossie's apartment, which was beautiful, and I helped Ossie and his wife lift all the belongings into the flat, and helped him settle in.

Later that evening, I began the long journey back to London. Spurs could have used a courier company, but the club always preferred the personal touch, and they knew Ossie and I were friends, so it was a perfect way of saying that Spurs really cared about him. And after just one turbulent season in Paris, Ossie returned to Tottenham, helping us win the UEFA Cup in 1984. I will always look back on that journey to Paris with pride, because I was so happy to be trusted with such an important job.

A year on, in 1985, Johnny Wallis began to give me even more responsibility, finally letting me in on looking after the first-team kit, which had been a no-go for the first few years. He'd say, 'I've got too much on, can you do the first-team training kit?' Well, I was over the moon, having my hands on the first-team kit for the first time.

The next time that I was sat in the office with David Pleat and Johnny Wallis was five years later, and I was about to be offered the job of first-team kit manager. 'I've done a lot of years,' said Johnny solemnly, his face now really showing his age. 'I don't need the travelling and the responsibility any more.'

It was a sad moment, yet at the same time an incredibly exciting one. David agreed that I should take over, but for the time being with Johnny working alongside me, as my assistant, to bed me in. It was, as the saying goes: 'The father becomes the son, and the son becomes the father.' We agreed that Johnny would work just one last game looking after those famous lily-white shirts: the 1987 FA Cup Final against Coventry.

CHAPTER 4

'WHERE'S YOUR HOLSTEN?'

The alarm bells were ringing at Wembley Stadium. If you've ever been in the dressing room before an FA Cup Final at the Twin Towers, you'll know that shrill electric alarm that alerts the players that kick-off is just minutes away. The noise of the 98,000 singing fans filtered into the dressing room as the large blue door swung open, and the Tottenham Hotspur players lined up to step on to the pitch for their eighth appearance in the most famous of finals. But something was wrong.

'Where's your Holsten?' Clive Allen asked Glenn Hoddle, in an exchange that would become famous on the 'after-dinner' circuit for decades to come.

'Don't you think we should wait till after the game?' Glenn replied, oblivious to the fact that his shirt, like half of the team's, didn't have the name of our beer sponsor printed on it. The scandal would become one of the most talked about, and controversial, moments in the history of our lily-white shirt – and all on Johnny Wallis's last day.

I watched from the stands as the team trotted out on to the pitch, and stripped off their warm-up jackets to prepare for kick-off. I could tell instantly something was wrong, but I couldn't put my finger on it. Typically, Johnny had been his usual guarded self when it came to the first-team kit, and had personally sent the shirts off to have the words 'FA Cup Final, 1987' embroidered below the cockerel. What he somehow missed, after 30 years of looking after those shirts, was that only half of them carried the name of the beer brand that had paid us hundreds of thousands of pounds to be seen on the players' chests during the biggest televised game of football of the year.

I tried to get down to the pitch from my place in the stands and tell someone, but I think they already knew. And, if I got there, what would I do? We played the game in those shirts and we were beaten by Coventry in a tough game. The score remained 2–2 until full-time and went into extra time, and then, six minutes in, the unfortunate Gary Mabbutt scored an own goal after Lloyd McGrath centred the ball. It took an evil deflection off Gary's knee and over his own keeper, Ray Clemence. To that day, it was the only FA Cup Final in history that Spurs lost, and I think Glenn actually *needed* a beer by the end of the game. But remarkably, the shirt disaster got so much press it became possibly the best advertising that Spurs and Holsten ever had. They were debating it on television, in the newspapers... and a rival beer brand even mentioned it in an advertising campaign. It was the stunt that refreshed parts that other marketing ideas couldn't.

But for Johnny, I was heartbroken. It's every kit man's nightmare to make a mistake – and especially at a cup final, worse luck. It's the kind of thing you dread, and, for it to happen to Johnny on his last day, after three decades of absolute dedication to detail and an obsessive attention to perfection, it was the worst last day of a career you could possibly imagine.

We'd also been knocked out of the Football League Cup in the semi-finals, and had finished third in the league, and so, having spent most of the season challenging for a unique domestic Treble, we had ended up desperately empty-handed.

I officially took over as kit manager during the weeks following that ill-fated final. On the Monday morning, we were devastated, not only because of the mishap with the shirts, but also about the result. No one would ask Johnny any questions, out of respect. It was just a terrible accident, but a few weeks later I summoned the courage to ask him, not just out of curiosity, but also out of a genuine fear of repeating the same mistake.

'We had some shirts made up for the youth team,' Johnny sighed, 'and because these lads are not 18 years old, it's illegal for them to advertise an alcoholic brand.'

He explained that somehow the blank shirts had found their way into the bag on the way to the embroiderers, and by the time they arrived at Wembley it was just too late to do anything about it. 'It's just one of those things,' he said to me, touching me on the shoulder. 'Hopefully, it'll never happen to you.'

I was now in the hot seat myself and preparing for my first games as first-team kit manager, terrified of anything of the same magnitude ever going wrong. I'd been in charge only once before, when Johnny was taken ill back in 1984. We were playing Everton away, and, on the Friday morning before the game, the manager said to me, 'Go home and get your kit, you're going to Goodison.' We stayed at a hotel on Merseyside, and the night before the game Graham Roberts knocked on my door and told me he needed some kit to go for a run. Without having any training kit handy, I gave him the reserve goalkeeper shirt, a horrendous yellow number that thankfully we rarely used. 'There you go, mate,' I said cheerily.

When we got to the ground the next morning, I was a bag of nerves. Tottenham's most famous players were asking for spare studs, bigger shorts, smaller shorts, and I had a real sweat on. Then all of a sudden Ray Clemence came over and said, 'Where's the yellow jersey, Roy?'

Suddenly, a streak of fear ran down my spine. Roberts had sweated in it the night before and it was still wet and smelly. I explained what had happened, and Clem threw on the green one and had some choice words for me.

I thought, 'Oh fuck, now I'm in trouble,' but, just

before kick-off, Clem confessed that he saw Robbo running past his hotel window in the yellow shirt the night before, and they had both conspired to wind me up. Typical – it was 'wind up the new boy' time, but I was glad in a way that I had been broken in before my first official game in charge, which was in the 1988/89 season.

My responsibilities at home were also about to increase, as, shortly after getting the job, my first daughter, Vikki, was born. Everything was happening at once: my wife, new daughter and I moved from Edmonton to Cheshunt, where I bought my first house, near the new Spurs training ground. We bought a puppy as well, a beautiful bearded collie called Oliver. In the space of six months, I had gone from being reserve kit man to full-time kit manager, and I had a wife and daughter, a house and a dog.

Of course, the new job put a lot of pressure on my young family, with my working schedule changing from being at home all the time to always being away with the team as we concentrated on the First Division season of 1988/89. I would get home after a long shift of lifting piles of white shirts to find piles of dirty nappies, and my being away was certainly an added pressure on my wife, who had a newborn baby and no driving licence.

Everything was exhilarating but at the same time overwhelming. I used to look back at Johnny, who would take it all in his stride. Nothing ever fazed him, and, in my obsession to be as great as him, I was forever working. The quantity of kit increased, while the number of players and staff tripled. We had more and more teams, and by the early 1990s I started looking after all the kits, from the U8s up to the first team. The youth team set up at Tottenham had become big business, with the club keen to nurture young talent in the area, and keep up with the youth scheme at neighbouring clubs like Arsenal.

The result was Tottenham teams going all the way down to seven-year-old boys, managed by ex-players like Jimmy Neighbour. It was a forward-thinking move for the club, but the intensity of the work increased for me. Just the U10 team had thousands of pieces of kit – 20 pairs of socks, 20 shorts, 20 shirts – and the kids' teams would have endless numbers of substitutes. From the U18s up, they had as much training kit as the first team, with coats, jackets and all sorts. Monday mornings now made White Hart Lane look like a Chinese laundry, and I was struggling to keep up.

I didn't even get a pay rise. To be honest, I wasn't fussed about the money, it was all about the honour of working with the first team, who at the time were formidable. We'd signed Bobby Mimms, Paul Walsh and Terry Fenwick to strengthen a side clearly missing Glenn Hoddle, who, like Johnny Wallis, had left Spurs after that Coventry Cup Final.

They did give me a raise later that year, once I'd proved I could do the job, but I certainly didn't ask for one. Johnny had helped me order the kits for pre-season 1988/89, and for a few weeks before the season he helped me settle in. The staff used to come back from the summer break a week earlier than the players, and sort out the deliveries. Then, on 1 July 1988, I took over, and it was nerve-wracking. The apprentices came back on the 3rd or 4th, so it wasn't much of a summer holiday, even in those days – just three weeks, and it wasn't enough for Johnny, who was now quite unwell.

For his services to his country and to football, my cantankerous predecessor Johnny Wallis was rewarded in the Queen's Birthday Honours List, making him Johnny Wallis MBE. This recognition, I feel, was thoroughly warranted and deserved.

For the first 12 or so games that I was in charge, I used to hide in my kit room on match days. There was a big door, and I would stand behind it and only speak when I was spoken to. I took a real back seat, because I was as new to them as they were to me. I changed studs if they needed it, but I deliberately kept my head down.

I always used to like listening to manager David Pleat's team talks, but always from the safety of my kit room. David had his own way of expressing himself, and his knowledge of football was encyclopaedic: any footballer, any division, he could tell you how much they weighed, if they kicked with a left or right foot and what they had for breakfast.

But as the months and years wore on, I began to feel part of the team. I can't explain why, but, when they were getting a bollocking, I felt it too. Defeats used to hurt when I was a supporter, but now I was part of the team, and in the dressing room, it was personal. Occasionally, you'd get big rows, with managers biting at players or players shouting at each other. As anyone who's ever played in any kind of competitive team will tell you – from Sunday league to Premiership – at half-time and you're 2–0 down, it's going to kick off. The dressing room filled with arguments, players fought at half-time then came back in at full-time celebrating and hugging each other like it had never happened.

Seasons came and went and so did the shirts, with the kit manufacturers changing from Hummel to Umbro to Adidas, with many other smaller brands in between, but, as ever, that blue cockerel remained proud, stitched in right above the heart. Players came, scored, threw their dirty socks on the floor and left. The shorts got longer, as did the haircuts, and Spurs were once again the formidable force they were when I was a youngster.

David Pleat had departed in October 1987, but good news was to follow as Terry Venables was hired. Terry had just guided Barcelona to the Spanish League title and European Cup Final. He arrived to make Spurs the same kind of successful outfit, and promised big signings that would make Tottenham Hotspur a formidable force in English football. But we had no idea that one of Terry's signings would change the club forever.

CHAPTER 5
GAZZA, GUNS AND GOALS

In his autobiography, Alex Ferguson claimed that the biggest disappointment in his managerial career was 'not getting Gazza'. Instead of Manchester United, the Geordie midfielder was wooed into signing for Terry Venables and Tottenham Hotspur in 1988 for a then British transfer record of £2m. Just two years later, he would explode on to the international football scene, becoming a household name in the World Cup in 1990, before making his name for Spurs in 1991, with an equally brilliant and tragic performance in the FA Cup. Two million quid was a bargain, I think. Because Tottenham Hotspur got a superstar – and I got a new friend. In the space of a few years, Paul Gascoigne and I became very close.

On one of Paul's earliest pre-season tours to Scandinavia, we'd been given a day off and the local guide laid on golf, sightseeing and various pastimes to keep the players entertained for an afternoon.

'Have you got any fishing?' Gazza had enquired, and immediately I knew we were kindred spirits. So me, and the other Spurs fishermen, Paul Stewart and Steve Sedgley, were given some fly-fishing rods and a lift to a nearby lake. Me, Stewy and Sedge hadn't fly-fished before, but Gazza was a seasoned fly-fisherman and very talented. He was casting out 20 metres further than we were, and, although he hadn't been at the club long, I remember noticing it was one of the only times I'd ever seen him calm, such was his usual energy and enthusiasm.

We stood on that bank, fishing for an hour, and that hour became two hours, and still we'd not had a single bite. Gazza was getting restless. Then all of a sudden we saw this other fella out in a boat, and he was catching loads of fish! Gazza was watching him reel in fish after fish, filling his net with some amazing-looking specimens. We were all getting mightily annoyed, and stared out at the lake where our flies remained motionless on the water. Then, suddenly, we heard, 'Way aye, I've got one!'

Gazza wasn't anywhere to be seen. We looked up and down the lake, and then we saw him, submerged in the water, fully clothed, and reeling in a huge fish, over his head. All you could see was his hair!

Gazza waded back to the shore with this fish above his head like the FA Cup, and we took it back to the hotel, where the chef cooked it up and Gazza presented it to Terry Venables for his tea. It was the freshest fish he'd ever tasted. This episode was an early glimpse of Paul Gascoigne's typically bizarre behaviour. As I was to learn in the coming years, when Gazza was involved, more often than not he'd find himself right up to his neck in it.

Of course, I knew about Gazza from his Newcastle days. I'd seen the photo of Paul having his nuts squeezed by Vinnie Jones, and I knew that he was one of the most highly rated young players in the country. But at Spurs you learned never to accept anyone was going to sign till they walked through the door. People often ask me, 'Who was the best player you had at Spurs?' and I could list hundreds: Perryman, Lineker, Klinsmann, Ginola... I mean, Glenn Hoddle could drop a ball on a sixpence (although he preferred Tony Galvin's right foot), and Jürgen was a goal machine. And Ossie had outrageous skills. But the greatest player I ever put in a Spurs shirt was Paul Gascoigne. He had this fantastic lunging run and two great feet. He could drift past people, head it and tackle. Gazza also had a heart as big as a dustbin lid, and he just didn't know when he was beaten: kick him and he'd get up and laugh at you, and pull that famous stupid face. I watch football today and the game has got quicker, the training and conditioning are better, but I believe if Gazza was playing today he'd still be one of the best players in the world. What's more, he was tremendous fun to have around.

I remember when he first signed for Spurs, Gazza found a 'run-around' guy called John Coberman. John was a Jewish boy who used to do a lot of running around for all the guys, but Gazza took him under his wing, and he used to help the player in various ways. One day at the training ground in Mill Hill, Gazza turned up with a massive motorhome that he'd bought for his father. Being Gazza, he'd bought a top-of-the-range, big American jobby, and when he drove into the ground everyone was amazed – we'd never seen anything like it. Then he told John that there was some kind of rattle from up on the roof and, without question, John was climbing up there to check it out.

But it was all a ruse, and Gazza quickly started the engine and backed it out of the drive, put his foot down and sped down Page Street towards McDonald's. The last we saw of the vehicle, it was tearing round the corner and poor John was clinging on for his life! Gazza drove all the way down to the M1, and when he finally returned, I've never seen anyone look as ill as John. He was as pale as a milk bottle! But that was to be just the first of a million pranks Gazza would play at Tottenham. He became famous for them.

He'd regularly burn Erik Thorstvedt's clothes; every morning he'd set fire to them, because he used to say that Norwegians had no dress sense. So Erik used to take three sets of training kit a session from me, which was a nightmare. He'd come in wearing one set, put one on to train in, and go home in another, just to save his clothes from being burned to ashes by Paul Gascoigne!

I got to know Gazza very closely around the riverbeds

and lakes of North London. He was an awful loser and, at the same time, a great winner. Be it football or fishing, he wasn't happy unless it was in the net. And if the result didn't go his way, he'd stomp around, throw things on the floor and mope for days. It became clear to me that Paul thought he could win every game – be it Barnsley in the cup or United at Old Trafford, he believed he could win it single-handedly and, more often than not, he did.

Under Terry Venables, Gascoigne developed into a world-class footballer. His powerful physique allowed him to hold off defenders and weather all challenges, and in his first season at White Hart Lane he helped Spurs to sixth in the First Division, and to third position the following season. Over those two seasons, he made a total of 75 appearances in all competitions, scoring 14 goals, many of them remarkable. A couple were frankly unbelievable.

Gazza was also one of the liveliest players I'd ever had in my dressing room. He'd come in before a game, playing pranks, even on match days. He'd come in at half-one, pull his shorts up to his armpits and loon around. But then, just as suddenly, he'd turn into 'Gazza the footballer'. He'd be zoned in, he'd do his warm-up, score three goals and come back in and start messing around again.

Gary Lineker and Gazza became close when we signed Gary from Barcelona in 1989. Gary was the polar opposite to Paul: aloof, a bit of a gentlemen and somewhat distant, unlike his alter ego on the television and those crisp adverts. Gary used to grab Gazza and say, 'Calm yourself down, this is a big game.' Even in those early days, Gary kept his eye on Gazza out on the pitch, which the whole nation later witnessed at the World Cup in 1990, when a booked Gazza turned to tears, and Gary pointed to the bench to alert the manager that Gazza was in trouble. Venables, Gazza's manager at Tottenham, was the best man-manager I've worked with, but, to talk to Gazza, he might as well have been talking to the wall.

We used to have a secretary called Irene at our Mill Hill training ground, and she had a big soft spot for Gazza. He used to take the mickey out of her something rotten. One day, he came out of the dressing room stark naked and went to her office, saying, 'Irene, have you got a towel?' Now, why would Irene have a towel! It was just to embarrass her. Irene said, 'Gazza, put it away and go inside. I don't find you funny!' Every day was like this. Every day he'd find something or somehow to wind someone up. He'd put Deep Heat in people's pants, and he'd find it so funny. Gazza needed to be loved, but sometimes I thought he worked too hard at it. He was a folk hero among the staff, although Terry Venables and his assistant Alan Harris would often be pulling their hair out.

In the old days, when you walked into the main reception area at White Hart Lane, there was a reception on the left-hand side, where a receptionist would sit answering the phones. One day I was walking through reception

SHIRTS, SHORTS & SPURS

with Gazza on the way to training, when he suddenly jumped behind the desk, and took the headset off the girl. He calmly sat down, put on the headset, and started taking calls. It was hilarious! He'd pick up a call and say, 'Way aye! Tottenham Hotspur, how can I help yous?' Every call he'd say, 'Of course, I'll pop you through,' and push them through to all departments. He said, 'It's free tickets today! I'll put you through.' The poor receptionist was terrified she'd lose her job, but, as usual, Gazza got away with it and everyone found it really funny.

Once, we were fishing in a local lake in Hoddesdon called Harry's Lake, which was right near Gazza's house, and it had all kinds of species in it. I used to fish it regularly with Gazza, and the fishing became a real bond between us. One day it was me, my pal Mark Beels, Paul Stewart, Sedge and Gazza all fishing on our day off. Now, with Gazza, you couldn't tell him when you were packing up, because, if you said it was 5pm, he'd clown around for the last hour, throwing stones and the like, because Gazza's attention span was awful.

Well, after just a few minutes, he said to me, 'Roysie, can I borrow your car?' Now, lending Gazza anything was a risky business, but I handed over my keys and heard him roar off in the direction of some nearby shops. Gazza being Gazza, he returned with a carrier bag full of sweets and chocolate. You couldn't close the handles it was so full, and among other treats was a big tin of biscuits. Gazza went over to an old boy who was fishing next to us, held the bag open and politely said to this old guy, 'Do you fancy a biscuit?' Well, this man reached into the bag and took the entire box, and stuck it under his chair, and said to Gazza, 'Thank you very much, young man, I'll enjoy them this evening!' Gazza was spitting feathers! He was so annoyed! He spent the rest of the day throwing stones at the bloke's float, making sure he didn't catch anything.

It was remarkable that Gazza's pranks never got him into more trouble, but one day at White Hart Lane he nearly came a real cropper. It was a Friday night and Gazza came in and decided he wanted to shoot the pigeons in the East Stand. Jimmy Five Bellies, his famously rotund pal, was there too, which always meant trouble. Gazza had climbed up on the rafters with an air rifle and was shimmying along towards a pigeon. He didn't want to just shoot it; he wanted to blow it to smithereens. Just as he was inches away, and Gazza gently started to squeeze the trigger, suddenly the pigeon flew into life and flapped away! It totally shocked Gazza who fell off the roof with an awful thump. Jimmy dragged him over to the dressing room, wounded. He arrived in my dressing room bleeding and bruised, and we called the physio right away to patch him up so he could play the next day. Of course, we had to keep it a secret from Terry Venables.

That wasn't the only time Gazza brought his rifle to work. He used to take aim at my kit-room door from 20 metres, shooting targets he'd stuck on the door. You could see the pellet holes for years to come. He'd say,

'Jimmy, go and pick up a pair of shorts for me,' and, when Five Bellies crossed the dressing room, Gazza would try to shoot him up the arse! It could get a little distracting when you were trying to sort out the kit for the next day's game, with shots flying around!

In a way, Gazza was like a little boy, but I really enjoyed his company. We'd play staff games on a Monday night, and occasionally we'd invite local Sunday teams to play us. Our team would include players like Micky Hazard and John Moncur, as well as staff members like Andy Church. Sometimes, if Gazza was doing a coaching session on the Monday, he couldn't resist joining in, and suddenly you'd have England International Paul Gascoigne playing in a five-a-side in the gym. And Gazza being Gazza, he couldn't just take it easy, he was playing to win, even against pub teams, and was always ringing wet with sweat!

I remember after one such game, Gazza had on a white tracksuit and it was soaked with sweat. So he took it off and said to me, 'Can you give me a lift home, Roysie? I haven't got a car.'

He lived not far away from me in Broxbourne, so I agreed to take him home but I told him I had to drop something off to my mum on the way. We got in the car, Gazza in just his pants, and, as I was backing down my mum's little cul de sac, suddenly Gazza got out of the car. He ran up and knocked on the door, and, when my mum answered, he said, 'I'm with Roy, and can I have a drink, please!'

I was racing up the drive after him, but he was much too quick. Gazza was in there, half-naked, going through the cupboards pulling out drinks! My mum used to call him 'Garza', and I'll never forget the look on her face when I finally got to the front door. Mum was stood in the doorway, wide-eyed, and she said, 'Garza's in the kitchen!'

Whether it was a five-a-side ball-court match, a training-ground game, a first-team game or an England International, Paul Gascoigne played with the same energy and eagerness to win. I used to say that you needed two balls when he was playing: one for Gazza, and one for the rest of the team. I lost count of the times I watched Gazza pick the ball up in his own 18-yard box and drift past three players. Before you knew it, he was bearing down on goal. He was simply terrific and so strong he'd just shrug people off. His best goal, of course, was his 1991 FA Cup semi-final free-kick against Arsenal.

A few years earlier, the same fixture – the 1989 semi-final between Liverpool and Nottingham Forest – was played at Hillsborough, Sheffield, but the game famously turned to tragedy when 96 supporters were killed in the stands due to overcrowding. The Hillsborough disaster had wide-ranging effects on the game, with the FA moving to ban standing up at matches, and, as a consequence, they were keen to make sure this heated London derby, between Spurs and their long-hated rivals

Arsenal, was played in the proper arena. They booked Wembley, the national stadium, more akin to hosting finals and Internationals, for the job. And the match was to live up to all expectations, with a four-goal thriller and one of the finest moments in Tottenham's history.

Five minutes into the game, I was settling down next to Terry Venables on the bench to enjoy the game, and Gazza was placing the ball down for a free-kick. Now, what people forget is that Gazza had just had his double hernia operation, so we didn't know if he was going to play, let alone last the game. He'd missed the last few matches and he was cramping up just before that free-kick. He must have been 40 yards out, and I remember there was a huddle of players who all broke away, and of course there was a long red wall in his way.

'Is Gascoigne going to have a crack?' the commentator asked a television audience of several million. 'He *is*, you know.'

But the millions at home, the 77,893 fans in the crowd and even the nervous Arsenal wall meant nothing to Gazza. This was a moment between Paul Gascoigne and David Seaman. We all knew Gazza could hit the ball, but I remember Terry shouting from the bench, 'Don't shoot! Don't shoot!' But Gazza was taking a massive run-up. 'Don't shoot!' Terry pleaded, from the bench, rising to his feet. But Gazza sprinted towards the ball and Terry's shout of 'Don't...' turned into: 'Great goal!'

Gazza came running towards the crowd and the bench, absolutely ecstatic. It was one of the greatest goals ever scored at Wembley, perhaps one of the finest free-kicks in history. And whether or not it's true, I've heard some players recall that Gazza said to Seaman as he arced away in celebration: 'Don't go for *them*.'

It was such a relief, as this was a huge game against our hated rivals, Arsenal. They were formidable, and there was also a big rivalry between George Graham and Terry Venables, the managers who had played in the same Chelsea team years back. I was ever the optimist, but, when I looked at it on the day, we had a great team but Arsenal were strong: Seaman, Adams, Winterburn, Dixon – they were a proper team who'd been playing together for years. I knew we'd need something magical to beat this lot, and Gazza provided it. Venables admitted later that the free-kick was a goal only Gazza could score. 'It was surely the best we've ever seen in the history of the competition,' Terry told a newspaper. 'Not only did he bend and lift it, he hit it with incredible power. I can't think of another player who could have done it.'

With his seventh goal of the tournament, Gazza had more or less got us to Wembley single-handed. He could turn it on against anybody, be it Oxford United or Arsenal. You see, Gazza didn't know the difference between playing United or Shrewsbury. Next, Gary Lineker made it 2–0 inside ten minutes with a typical poacher's goal that was scrambled over the line after some confusion in the Arsenal penalty box. But while Arsenal fought back with a headed goal from Alan Smith before half-time, and despite retaining possession in the second half, they never truly looked like scoring again. Lineker booked Tottenham's return ticket to Wembley for the final with a glorious solo effort – cutting through the Arsenal team like a hot knife through butter, from the halfway line to the box, before unleashing a powerful shot that was too hot for Seaman to handle. Spurs were in seventh heaven. 'I'm off to get me suit measured!' a beaming Gazza told the TV cameras, as Spurs were to return to Wembley to play Brian Clough's Nottingham Forest in the final.

After the World Cup in 1990 in Italy, Gazza-mania was born. Paul had lit up the tournament with some dazzling displays as England reached the semi-finals, but it was in that infamous game with West Germany that Gazza became a legend: a mistimed foul on Thomas Berthold earned him a booking that would rule him out of the final, and those famous tears began to stream down his cheeks. It was a pattern that was to repeat itself: a flash of genius marred by a moment of madness.

'Is there anything else from this young man left to surprise us?' The commentator had rasped, as Gazza sprinted away from his marvellous free-kick. And it was to be a prophetic line, as the FA Cup Final was to become a tragic day for my friend Paul Gascoigne.

CHAPTER 6

A BITTERSWEET VICTORY

There were 39 steps to be climbed before one reached the imposing heights of Wembley's Royal Box after a cup final at the famous Twin Towers. They used to say that, if you were collecting a loser's medal and not a trophy, it felt like 300. Tottenham Hotspur had already climbed to great heights, teetering on the edge of going out of business during this cup run. Our road to Wembley had been a dizzying run of spectacular wins at home and away punctuated by flashes of brilliance by one player, Paul Gascoigne. On 18 May 1991, the scene was set for what was to be the most dramatic game of his career. The setting was perfect: Wembley was the first pitch to be referred to as 'Hallowed Turf', and there was a celestial burst of sunshine breaking through the clouds as Tottenham Hotspur and Nottingham Forest prepared to do battle in the 110th FA Cup Final.

We had stayed overnight at the Royal Lancaster Hotel in London, not only because it was a great hotel, but also because Terry Venables knew the manager. Always the entrepreneur was Terry. We trained on the Friday morning, jumped in the coach to the hotel and, after we dropped the lads off, I went on to Wembley and laid out the kit nice and early. The shirts would stay hung up all night, as I wanted to enjoy the day myself on Saturday, and, if anything was wrong, I'd notice in time to make changes. All the shirts were lovingly embroidered by Umbro with 'FA Cup Final, 1991', and I remember running my fingers over the embroidery, checking each and every shirt for imperfections. And I religiously made sure 'Holsten' was printed on every shirt!

Like Johnny Wallis before me, my mild OCD required everything to be absolutely right. That day at Wembley, the same as at White Hart Lane, the socks all had to face the right way, the hangers I put in the shirts all had to be facing the same way, too. As a kit man, you like to think you're part and parcel of the team, and while you can't change anything on the pitch, or alter the score, what you can do is the job to the best of your ability – and make the dressing room look the best. If the shirts are lined up perfectly, then the lads feel special and, in my mind, you've done your bit. On this Wembley Cup Final day, I was as nervous as the players, for this was to be the biggest day of my career so far.

I'd worked at Wembley with Spurs in 1988, at the ill-advised Makita Tournament, which was the forerunner of the now *de rigueur* tournaments that teams take part in every summer. Only that year it was to be held at the home of English football, Wembley Stadium. A ticket for the day cost just £6, but just 30,104 bothered to turn up, filling less than a third of the stadium. We didn't even get a dressing room, instead we had to lug the skips up a staircase and get changed with the marching band in a cramped room. But it was still Wembley, and it instilled in me a burning desire to get there on more competitive terms.

1991 would become that year, but, back at the hotel, someone was more excited than me. Gazza was worryingly hyperactive, and he couldn't sit still. He was so pumped up that the doctor had to give him a couple of sedatives to calm him down and get him to sleep. The next morning, the day of the final, everyone was buzzing. There were TV cameras in the hotel and fans were being interviewed, telling reporters that today was the day, and, famously, that the year ended in 'one' and that victory was written in the stars.

Making our way to the stadium was amazing, driving right down the old Wembley Way in the team coach, which I remember was sponsored by Joe Bloggs Clothing. It was sensational, and thinking about that journey sends shivers down my spine.

When we arrived at the stadium everything was set up just so, and Security had kept a close eye on the dressing room all night. I could breathe a sigh of relief as I checked the kit for the hundredth and final time. But Gazza was uncontrollable again, and we couldn't get him to sit down. It was like someone had wound him up with a key. When he got out on the pitch to warm up, he was trying to smash balls at the marching band, trying to knock their busbies off. It sounds funny, but with Gazza you wouldn't expect anything less. He used to tackle the away mascots when we played away from home, and, on this day, at 2.40pm he had his match shirt on and was stomping around the dressing room, singing and shouting. We just couldn't get him to calm down.

He was pinging around the dressing room like a pinball, and every time Terry Venables started to give the team talk, Gazza would jump in and shout, 'Come on, lads!' Terry kept trying to get Gazza to sit down, but he couldn't get a word in. In the end Terry sighed and said, 'Fuck it! Just go out there and play.' It was quite funny, I suppose. We all knew we had to let him go and do his thing. Even in the tunnel Gazza was taking the mickey out of the opposition and mugging for the cameras. And then that moment came when you must walk out on to the pitch.

Let me tell you, walking out at Wembley is an amazing experience. It's a strange sensation – when you're in the tunnel you can only see the far end of the crowd, and they can't see you in the shadows. As you walk purposefully up the tunnel, those fans at the end can now see the teams, and they explode into a low cheer which reverberates around the stadium as if it were a coliseum. I was trying to talk to the physio next to me, and we were side-by-side and we couldn't hear each other. We just looked each other and fell silent, taking in this most magnificent of moments. Lady Diana was there to meet the teams, and she was dazzling. She was so beautiful – very tall, elegant and suave, adding to the magic of the occasion.

Famously, Gazza made the Princess blush by kissing her hand. When Diana took her seat in the Royal Box, the teams lined up to kick off, and by now the noise was deafening. It was so different to the semi-final: louder, more frenzied, and we now knew we had a chance at winning the cup. I remember looking at Brian Clough, in his celebrated green jersey, and it all seemed like a dream.

As soon as the whistle blew, Gazza was like a man possessed, running around like a schoolboy. I think Terry was concerned because he'd laid out a structure for us to play, and Gazza was a loose cannon. We were all willing him to calm down, but it was like trying to control a wild steer.

In winning the ball out on the right touchline, with just three minutes gone, Gazza followed through with his foot up and caught Forest's Garry Parker square on the chest, branding the England player with six stud marks. No two ways about it, it was a bad foul, and I say to this day it should have been a booking. Referee Milford let him off with a lecture, and I believe that, if he had booked Gazza, he would have forced him to calm down.

But the early warning had not sunk in and at the 14th minute I watched as Gazza ploughed into Forest player Gary Charles in a moment that changed his life forever.

The Forest defender ran across the face of the Spurs penalty area, and it was one of those challenges where you have to look away. Gazza just scythed him down and it was horrendous. His knee whipped back the wrong way, and next to me on the bench Spurs physio Dave Butler jumped off the bench, his face etched with concern. I'd never seen Gazza stay down after a challenge. He was stupid and robust, and I saw some horrendous tackles on him over the years, and he always got up. When I looked at him, Gascoigne was motionless, and I thought, 'This is a problem.'

Eventually, he got back to his feet and Forest were awarded a free-kick on the edge of the box. After much treatment, and a yellow card that could have arguably been red, Gazza joined the defensive wall. But when Nottingham Forest's captain, Stuart Pearce, took the dead ball kick, Glover pulled Gary Mabbutt off the end of the wall and the ball flew past Thorstvedt to give Forest the lead in the 16th minute.

I couldn't keep my eyes off Gazza. When I did my own knee years ago – the injury that ended any hopes of me playing professionally – I remember I had excruciating pain, but then I stood up and felt fine for a minute. I watched as Gazza hobbled around, and then it happened. His ligaments had gone, and he collapsed, tragically, on to the cold, 'hallowed' Wembley turf. The day was over for him, and Terry brought on Nayim as Spurs set about getting back into the game.

After 25 minutes, Gary Lineker had a goal crucially cancelled out for offside, although he clearly was onside, and then, five minutes later, he was in on Mark Crossley, when the keeper brought him down in the box. He was awarded a penalty, yet no red card, leading me to wonder if the referee had left his red cards at home! Up stepped Lineker and put the ball to the keeper's left, but Crossley somehow kept the ball out. I crashed back down to my seat, deflated. I couldn't help but feel that perhaps this wasn't our day.

After the half-time break, an early goal was desperately needed to get Spurs back into the match, but we were struggling to defend and David Howells had to save us, clearing the ball off the line from Roy Keane's effort. The goal we were praying for came ten minutes after the break when Nayim, Gazza's replacement, found Paul Allen who put Paul Stewart in on the right-hand side of the box and he thrashed a low shot that hit the stanchion inside the net, causing Spurs fans to go ballistic. I remember Stewart jumped over the hoardings and ran on to the running track in celebration. The fans were ecstatic.

After that, the final moved into extra time, as both teams refused to commit to attacking for fear of losing to a late goal. With the game even at the end of 90 minutes, Brian Clough had retreated to the tunnel beneath the

Royal Box, while Venables continued to holler at the team from the pitch-side. I was glued to my seat, and gripped it with white knuckles, my nerves shattered. Paul Walsh hit the bar and it bounced back only for it to be put behind by Stuart Pearce for a corner, and the entire bench and the 35,000 Spurs fans had their hearts in their mouth. Nayim took the corner kick in the 94th minute; the ball floated over and Stewart met it perfectly; and Gary Mabbutt ran in at the far post, eager to head it home. But Forest defender Des Walker beat him to it and buried the ball past his own keeper. Tottenham, the underdogs, were in the lead for the first time in the game.

I'd forgotten I was working at this point. I was a supporter, jumping around, shouting and cheering. I thought at the time that Mabbsy had headed it in, but then the scoreboard showed that it was Des. I knew Dessy when he was an apprentice at Spurs. He was very unassuming. He was very similar to Ledley King: no airs and graces, but quite brilliant. At that moment, I was actually quite sad for him. He must once have dreamed of scoring the winning goal for Spurs at the FA Cup Final, but to do so in such tragic circumstances must have been horrendous. The remainder of extra time failed to produce much of note and, against the odds, Tottenham Hotspur were to have their name engraved on the FA Cup for the eighth time.

Naturally, we were ecstatic about winning the game. Whether you're the head coach or the kit man, it's an amazing experience. We celebrated afterwards, did the lap of honour, and I got thrown in the bath, a cup final prank that was to become tradition. Then, all of a sudden, we thought... 'Gazza'. At the time we didn't know that he had been taken to hospital, and we all expected him to be in the dressing room when we poured in after the final whistle.

Terry had a reception planned, win or lose, but instead we went as a team with the cup to the hospital. We walked into the ward en masse, and there was Gazza, his match shirt hanging above his bed. He managed a wry smile but he was devastated and in pain. He didn't even get to collect his medal, but Mabbutt had brought it along for him. Gazza was obviously dosed up to the eyeballs with painkillers, and you could tell he was in some pain, but he was putting a brave face on it. After all, he'd got us to that final. I found it really difficult to leave him there, knowing that he wouldn't be involved in the celebrations. You see, Gazza did have a self-destruct button, but the situations he got himself in, be it shooting pigeons or a rash challenge, were all done with the greatest of intentions. He had a heart of gold and, in many ways, he didn't deserve all the trouble he landed himself in.

Sadly, it took the shine off what was one of the greatest days of my life. To walk out with the team with the cup, watching the lads wave to their family and friends, was brilliant. And for me, as in this entire story, I still felt like a supporter, a supporter with the greatest job in the world. My team had just won the biggest prize in English football, and picking up the cup felt amazing. It was surprisingly heavy, and I remember the base was heavier than the lid, and the top of the lid looked the worse for wear! You know the little spike thing? It wasn't perfectly straight. The little details you remember! Days afterwards, they brought the cup back to White Hart Lane and I took a nice photo of it with one of the cup final shirts. I never thought to keep any of the shirts, although perhaps I should have. Mementos didn't do it for me any more, after I gave away all my autograph books when I was 16. It's something people always ask me about, but I never kept any. I suppose it was like working in a sweet shop – you don't go home and eat wine gums – you can't stand the sight of them!

What I do have, and what no one can take away from me, are the memories. I have a photograph of me holding the FA Cup with a shirtless and triumphant Paul Walsh. I remember shaking hands with Brian Clough. Whenever someone does a Clough impression, they always say 'Young man!' and that's exactly what he said to me at that cup final. It was very strange! I admired Clough, and he was a great man.

One of our apprentices at Spurs had been at Forest and told us the story of the time that Brian Clough phoned the apprentices' room and asked one of them to get him a cup of tea, only to be asked who it was. 'My name is Brian Clough and I'm the manager of this football club,' he said.

With Gazza, during his Everton days.

Charity match – Spurs Staff v Parliaments

Spurs assistant kit manager Roy Reyland comes up against Ossie Ardiles who guested for the Parliamentary side.

Left: Clash of the titans: me versus Ossie at White Hart Lane in a charity match.

Below: The Norwegian 'Horribles' team photo, including a few legends. See if you can spot Georgie Best.

Above: Finally, I score for Spurs – at Brisbane Road in a benefit match held for London Transport.

Below: A staff game at Craven Cottage.

bove left: With my friend and Spurs groundsman Colin White, in 1978, my first year t Spurs.

bove right: Me with the UEFA Cup, after the European triumph in 1984.

elow: Roberts, Hoddle and Archibald, celebrating our FA Cup Semi Final win against Volves in 1981.

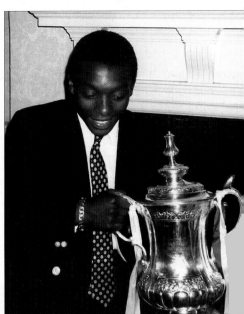

Above left: Stevie P's cup final speech at the Chanticleer banqueting rooms, next door to White Hart Lane, 1981.

Above right: I took this photograph of Garth Crooks with the FA Cup at the Town Hall.

Below: Me and Chrissy with the treasured Cup.

Spurs kit man of 22 years wins testimonial

FOOTBALL is a notoriously fickle business with players and managers sometimes changing clubs at an alarming rate.

But an exception to that trend is Roy Reyland, who is now celebrating 22 years service with Tottenham Hotspur.

Roy, from Brandon Close, Cheshunt joined Spurs as the kit man in 1976 when Keith Burkinshaw was manger.

His responsibilities include the everyday preparation of training kit for more than 30 players and coaching staff.

During his time at White Hart Lane, the 43-year-old has seen all the highs and lows of football.

"The good times include a number of visits to Wembley with the most recent being the 1991 FA Cup final victory over Nottingham Forest," said Roy.

Roy has also seen virtually every Tottenham game during his time with the club and is hard pushed to think of an all-time favourite match.

"I suppose I should say beating Arsenal in the FA Cup semi-final at Wembley," he said.

"But for drama and excitement it would have to be the FA Cup final replay against Manchester City with Ricky Villa's wonder goal."

In recognition of his 22 years with Spurs, Roy is holding a testimonial dinner at the Grosvenor House Hotel on Tuesday, October 21.

Tottenham's current team will be there along with former players and famous faces from the world of sport and television.

For more information and details of how to book places telephone 0171 722 9045, or write to HIT Limited, 51 Charlbert Street, London, NW8 6JN.

Roy Reyland has earnt his spurs

bove: Charity match at Spurs including Irvine Scholar, Tottenham chairman at the time.

low left: Me, my brother Terry (*centre right*) and the FA Cup, in the boardroom White Hart Lane.

low right: After 22 years at Spurs I even made the papers.

Ringing wet, having being dunked in the bath after defeating Leicester in the Worthington Cup final in 1999.

'Oh,' said the voice at the other end. 'And do you know who this is? You don't? Well, get your own fucking tea.'

And, as the story goes, the apprentices scattered down that corridor, running for their lives!

Some people later criticised Clough for leaving England International Steve Hodge on the substitutes' bench for that final, but I don't think he would have made a difference. In many ways – not just with the year ending in one – this was Tottenham's final. But the game had also scuppered Gazza's transfer to Lazio, who refused to take a crocked player to Italy, and instead he had to stay behind for rehabilitation, to make himself fit before the move. I was glad because it meant he stayed at Spurs that bit longer, even though that tragic cup final would be his last ever game in a Spurs shirt.

When Gazza had his knee operation, my eldest daughter Vikki was five, and we used to go round to his house and Vikki used to play videogames with him. I'd come in and they'd both be sat on the floor playing games, him in plaster. It was a funny sight. At the training ground, Gazza picked a small team of apprentices who would stay back after training and help him rehabilitate. There were probably about half-a-dozen boys, and in truth they were probably enjoying just training with Paul Gascoigne, but, when the time came for Gazza to finally leave Spurs, he drove down to the local bank and drew out as much cash as he could, and handed it all out to these young lads. It might not have been a fortune, but it was enough to make these young trainees very happy for a few months. That was the kind of guy he was. I was so very sad when he finally left. I felt like it was a massive loss to the club.

We returned to Wembley in 1993, to play Arsenal once again in the FA Cup semi-final. But it wasn't the same without the outrageous talent of Paul Gascoigne and the mercurial leadership of Terry Venables. Arsenal came out on top to gain sweet revenge, thanks to Tony Adams, who arrived at the far post with just 11 minutes left to knock us out of the cup. I remember the game was very tight, and, when Tony Adams made one of his famously late runs, I thought, 'If I can see him, surely someone else will, and mark him!' But he was left unguarded, and that was it.

After the game, I went on to the pitch to console the players, and the first player I saw was Nicky Barmby who was close to tears. We walked off together, oblivious to the noise and cheers of the Arsenal fans, and Nicky said to me, 'That's it, Roysie, I'll never play at Wembley again.' It was a poignant moment, and one that was captured from afar by a photographer with a long lens. I'll always cherish that moment. That photo says a lot about football. Anyone who thinks footballers get paid too much and don't care about results – look at the anguish on Nicky Barmby's face. Nobody likes to lose to his arch rivals, but this match was different. Without Gazza's magic, it was clear we couldn't and shouldn't have progressed to the final, where Arsenal beat Sheffield Wednesday.

Paul Gascoigne was the best I've ever seen in a Spurs shirt, and to this day he's my superhero. His private life is his private life, and, although I know he's had some turbulent times of late, I have the most admiration for him as a footballer and as a charitable man. I feel so, so sad for him when I read what is going on with him today. There were just too many outside influences, too many people around him that took his mind off the game. Of course, he recovered from that injury, but I think he lost half a yard of pace. I think we had the very best of Gazza at Spurs, and for that I'm grateful.

Years later, when Everton visited White Hart Lane in 2000, there was a knock at the dressing-room door, and there was Gazza, grinning away as usual. 'Hello, Roysie!' he said, embracing me. He asked how my daughter was, and we caught up briefly. It was strange seeing him without that famous cockerel on his chest, but it was just great to see him. He had his young son with him, and Gazza grabbed a nearby photographer and we had a photo together, one that I cherish. 'Legend' is a word that is often thrown around too easily, but Paul Gascoigne is the greatest player I've ever seen at Tottenham Hotspur Football Club.

For me, a taste of Wembley success had made me love my job, and Tottenham Hotspur, so much more. As a boy I had dreamed of lifting the FA Cup with Spurs, and in a roundabout way I had achieved my dream. I felt very much at home at Spurs, and was no longer hiding in my kit room on match days... I was part of the team and loving every moment. The night we passed round the FA Cup full of champagne, I decided that I would stay at Tottenham Hotspur as long as they would have me. I wanted a backroom career that would match that of Steve Perryman, who had notched up over 800 appearances. I wore my Spurs tracksuit with pride, and worked every day with the same enthusiasm I got from the players. Yes, we had bad seasons, and over the years I coped with shocking losses to minor teams, early exits from major tournaments, and all the disappointments that came with working with a top-flight team. But I loved every minute of it, because, for a boy from Edmonton, Tottenham Hotspur had given me a lifetime of experiences that I would never have achieved had I not accepted Johnny Wallis's job all those years ago.

CHAPTER 7
SPURS IN... BERMUDA?

You wouldn't believe the places Spurs have played pre-season friendlies: it's not always 'Bournemouth away'. In fact, our gruelling pre-season tours have taken me to countries I couldn't have even placed on a map. Places I certainly wouldn't have seen if I'd stayed working for that furniture factory in Tottenham, instead of joining the club.

'Bermuda?' moaned a voice from inside the laundry room. 'Why do we have to go to bloody Bermuda? What's wrong with England?' This was the voice of Johnny Wallis one day in 1986, and, typically, he was having a moan-up on a Monday morning. I had opened the door to find my mentor up to his knees in dirty shirts, complaining that he'd have to travel to a beautiful tropical island, free of charge, for a hastily organised

Tottenham Hotspur friendly. At the end of the 1986/87 season, Spurs were enjoying a League Cup run, had just survived a tough 3–3 draw with Manchester United at Old Trafford, and the team were seriously in need of a break. What's more, the temperature in London had dropped to a bitter minus-1 degree, and the weather, like Johnny, was rather changeable.

'I don't want to go,' sighed Johnny. 'Will you go instead, Roy?' he pleaded, passing me a mucky shirt.

I was flabbergasted. 'Well, yes, if they'll let me, of course I will!' I said keenly.

At the time, I'd never heard of Bermuda, as back then it wasn't the popular holiday destination it is today – it was a place only the mega-rich and famous travelled to, like John Lennon, who holidayed there in the 1980s.

David Pleat agreed I could go instead of Johnny, and take care of the kit. I was given a ticket to fly with the team, and I was over the moon.

I don't know what the connection was with Bermuda, but I remember a Spurs team had beaten a 'Bermuda Select XI' back in 1979, during a tour that included matches in Kuwait, Malaysia and Japan. In this previous encounter, Spurs goalkeeper Milija Aleksic played on the right wing and a number of the backroom staff also appeared in the team, including assistant secretary Peter Day and physiotherapist Mike Varney. I wondered whether I should bring my boots! Either way, as the sleet began to bucket down in North London, I was aboard the team plane, soaring high above the Atlantic.

The heat struck you like a brick wall as you stepped off the plane. The weather was tremendous, and Bermuda was the most glamorous place I'd ever been. It was as different to Edmonton as you could imagine. The locals were falling over themselves to help us, such was their generosity and politeness. We were treated like royalty, and the trip did the lads the world of good. There was very limited training in Bermuda, but the boys got some time off to play golf, and the staff went out briefly to see the sights. It's not big, Bermuda, only twice the size of Haringey, so we got round the whole island in one day. We played the match on the Tuesday in the blistering sunshine, and we won 3–1, with Clive Allen and Hoddle scoring and Waddle finishing off with a penalty. I remember working in just a T-shirt and shorts, such was the heat, and it was an amazing experience.

We returned after just four days, brown as berries. I remember sitting down to Christmas dinner, completely tanned. People were staring at me in the street, and they scarcely believed me when I said I'd been to Bermuda. It would serve as an early taste of what was to come, for, after I took over as first-team kit manager, Spurs made pre-season and end-of-season tours a regular thing. I would soon be working everywhere from Japan, to Hong Kong, to America and all over Scandinavia.

Scandinavia became a popular destination for Spurs, because there were great facilities. They were years ahead of us at the time, and their equipment and pitches were perfect – we learned a lot from the Scandinavians, in fact.

They'd done their homework at Tottenham, and figured out that it was just a two-hour flight to Sweden, Norway or Denmark, and these countries were really geared up for us. Plus, end-of-season tours became a financial money-spinner, and soon we'd end up playing in more exotic places like Miami. It became promotional, you see, and on these trips you tended to see more of the countryside, because the intensity isn't like the pre-season where players are trying to get match-fit.

People would always say to me, 'What was Korea like?' And I'd have to say, 'Well, the hotel was fine.' Because on pre-season tours, it's a serious business. And for me, the work was just as tough, as the team would be doing full training sessions, and that meant the full kit requirements. I'd have two hotel rooms, one for me and one that would become a temporary kit room. All the sights were wasted on me on pre-season tours, because I'd spend most of my time in the hotel laundry!

What I do remember about Korea was that the humidity was unbearable, and it was hard for the boys to train. You lost so much fluid even walking to the training pitch, let alone sprinting. When we arrived, I requested 20 footballs to train with, before we embarked on a cup competition out there, against the likes of Boca Juniors, Real Sociedad and French champions Lyon. I asked our liaison guy for the footballs, but he just pointed to 20 deflated ones. There was a language barrier, and instead of an electric pump he came back with just a hand pump. So, I pumped up those 20 balls in the terrible humidity...

and I nearly passed out! Sweat was pouring off me. But the trip was worth it and was a massive success. We won the competition, beating Lyon in a dramatic final in Seoul.

We had to wear a foreign logo on the front of our shirts, instead of our normal kit sponsor, so we had special kit made up for the occasion. It was becoming clear that trips to the Far East were increasingly important to the club, as the business side of things started to take off, particularly with selling replica shirts abroad. When we signed South Korean YP Lee from Dutch side PSV on 31 August 2005, manager Martin Jol touted him as 'the best left back in Holland, and one of the best left backs in Europe today'.

Lee certainly was a superb player, and, like that old cliché about Far Eastern players, he had a work ethic that far exceeded his ability. I remember when we signed Toda, our first Japanese player – a lovely chap, and again, a really hard worker. We really adapted to his cultures and traditions at Spurs. We would bow at each other, until one day I found out that he always had to bow lower than you, so every time at dinner I used to get down on my knees and bow, so he'd have to stop eating, and get right down on the floor!

We had a fun relationship.

When I decided to have my girls' names tattooed on my back in Japanese, I went to Toda to get the translation done. I wonder to this day what he really gave me as a translation, to get back at me for my bowing! I could have Tokyo telephone numbers on my back, as far as I know. Toda only played four games, but he was massively popular at White Hart Lane. When he arrived he asked me for the number 44 shirt, and I didn't argue. 'It's my favourite dish,' he joked, but later he confessed that it was just his lucky number.

When we stayed in Japan, the better-known players would get mobbed if we went out in public. But as you read about rock stars who visit Japan, the fans were always so polite. The bigger names would get dragged off from training to do bizarre TV and newspaper interviews, but the trips were also great for the younger lads. We'd always take a dozen young lads, because Spurs would play something like three games in ten days. Instead of 90 minutes, you'd play three periods of 30 minutes, because, although the idea is still to win, ultimately it's a fitness thing. And for the younger lads, seeing foreign cultures and traditions was a real eye-opener.

Now, I'm a bit of a plain Jane when it comes to food, and some of the things we were given in Japan I just couldn't stomach. Squid and octopus made me feel a bit funny – I don't eat anything with the suckers still on. But I always tried a bit of the cuisine, because it's important to show respect to your hosts. And while I stayed in some of the top hotels in the world, the players were in training so we would all get specially prepared food: rice, pasta, chicken... so I never got to eat a la carte like the rest of the diners. While it may sound that I'm complaining that the Champagne was too fizzy, I'm just saying I never ordered the lobster when I worked for Spurs!

One of my favourite trips with the Spurs team was when Christian Gross took us to St Moritz in Switzerland. St Moritz is considered one of the best winter resorts in the world, due to its favourable location up in the mountains and its record of 300 days of sunshine a year. It was also home to the most unbelievable hotel I've ever stayed in, and the training out in the fresh air was brilliant.

One afternoon we hired 30 mountain bikes and all of us cycled through the Alps, which was beautiful. It was a training exercise, so the team had to make it up a steep ascent, with the staff bringing up the rear. We were panting, for this hill was a punishing exercise in fitness. But we were just halfway up the mountain, when suddenly an old military truck overtook us on a bend and we had to pull in sharply to the side of the track. It was like one of those army trucks from *The Great Escape*, and it had a tarpaulin across the top. As it whizzed past, we saw a hand lift up the tarpaulin, and inside was a mountain bike, and Spurs midfielder Nicola Berti!

He'd paid the truck driver to drive him up to the top of the mountain and drop him off! He gave us a wink, and a cheeky wave, and pulled down the tarpaulin. At the top, he jumped out and cycled the last hundred metres. Needless to say, when he reached the top of the mountain that day, he looked like the fittest player in the squad – he'd hardly broken a sweat! Nicola Berti was a fine player, but unfortunately, like many of our better players at the time, we'd bought him at the end of his career.

Not all Spurs trips were so entertaining and the

locations were not always as picturesque. When we qualified for the 1999/2000 UEFA Cup, we were drawn against Zimbru Chişinău, a grim outfit based in Chişinău, Moldova. It was hardly the glamour tie we had all been imagining, as we celebrated our qualification for Europe. But on 30 September 1999, we made the journey to the landlocked country, wedged between the twin perils of Romania and the Ukraine. This game was situated quite literally between a rock and a hard place.

UEFA regulations state that you must land a minimum of 24 hours before the match, so we arrived at the hotel the night before the game, and, putting it politely, it was inadequate. We did a spot of training, had an evening meal the night before the game, and the players got their heads down nice and early. A little tradition of mine was that, wherever we went, I'd go for a 20-minute walk around town to walk off my dinner. If it were Middlesbrough or Mauritius, I'd go off on my own for a little stroll. However, in Moldova it was a different story. According to the CIA, widespread crime and underground economic activity were among the major issues in the country, and we had security guards with us everywhere we went.

Regardless, after my tea I said to the boys, 'I won't be long,' and walked towards the hotel door. I'd spotted a pleasant-looking square by the hotel and planned a couple of laps before bed. Suddenly, one of the Moldovan guards that had been quietly looking over us, stood between me and the door and said in broken English,

'Where you going?' I told him my plans, and he said sternly, 'I'll come with you.'

I said, 'Don't be silly, mate,' but, as I reached for the door, he opened his jacket, pulled out a pistol and cocked it, presumably so he would be ready to repel any attacker. I just looked at him, looked at the gun and said, 'You know what? I don't fancy a walk tonight!'

The next morning, as per my usual routine, I got down to the stadium nice and early. I found Zimbru Stadium to be a grim, concrete affair – 'ramshackle' would be the most flattering way to describe it. It was surrounded by imposing 10ft metal gates, and that day was guarded by militia with Alsatians the size of donkeys, straining at the leash. Now, I don't mind dogs, but these animals looked like real killers, and the atmosphere was far from friendly.

I asked someone, 'Where are the dressing rooms please?' and I was pointed towards an old closet door. I remember thinking, 'This must be a little alley leading to the dressing room.' But no, this *was* the dressing room! I opened the door and it was like stepping inside someone's living room. There was an old sofa, a flea-bitten armchair and some wooden chairs. Well, it really ruined my chi because I couldn't hang the shirts up in my normal organised way – in fact, there were no hangers at all. I remember laying David Ginola's shirt over the back of a knackered green settee and laughing to myself: 'I can't wait for the lads to see this!'

Just 7,000 people turned up to see that match, barely filling the stadium's 10,500 capacity. Ginola didn't even play that day, and we ground out a dull 0–0 draw. Later, we would be beaten by German team Kaiserslautern and knocked out of the tournament before we got near to playing some of the competition's more attractive sides.

During Ossie's reign, on a pre-season tour in southern Ireland, Stevie Perryman and myself were the only two left in the dressing room while the lads were warming up, when a elderly chap, who obviously worked at the stadium, came into the dressing room to collect the empty teacups. He looked at Stevie with a double-take, and said in his strong Irish brogue, 'Do you know who you used to be?'

Stevie looked at him strangely.

'You used to be Steve Perryman!'

To which Stevie replied, 'Who the fuck am I now then?'

It was a strange old day, and trips to Ireland were always punctuated with run-ins with strange characters, and this one was no different. Later, the old gentleman returned, and Stevie, playfully said to him, 'Can you tell me where the pitch is?' And the chap, not even turning his head, replied. 'Yeah, it's outside.'

At another game in Northern Ireland, we were warming up prior to a game when an announcement came over the speakers: 'This is an important announcement.' Everyone looked up. None of us knew what to expect and, this being during a time of great unrest, we listened up for what would come next: 'Bovril will be served at half-time.'

Travelling away with Spurs was always eventful, even if the game was just a few miles down the road. One time we were driving to the old Highbury stadium to play Arsenal away and, as we passed the Arsenal pubs in our posh THFC coach, a beer bottle flew into the windscreen, splintering into a thousand frothy pieces. It gave us all a hell of a jump, but I remember vividly that it was a bottle of Holsten Pils! I thought, 'Typical!'

Providing it's not violent, all this tension adds to the drama. At Highbury the away dressing room used to be right on the street; it felt like getting changed in my sister Jean's flat on Park Lane! Should one of the lads open the window, the torrent of abuse that would come through was deafening. I remember Chrissie Armstrong stuck his head out the window once, and the fans absolutely rifled him. It was the worst bit of abuse I've ever heard, and Chrissie just slipped down the wall and curled into a ball. It was hilarious!

And, of course, in all the years travelling abroad, there were bound to be a few mishaps – like turning up at a European hotel and finding we were one aluminium skip missing. I'd always count them on at the airport personally and I'd have a list and watch them put on to the plane. But somehow one skip had been left at Heathrow. It had nothing important in it – just the match shirts! We managed to get it flown over especially and it arrived at 12.05, before kick-off at 3pm. I had a sweat on that day.

Another time, when we were playing Brighton away in the cup, I opened my hotel door in the middle of the night to a worried-looking David Pleat. The team coach had been vandalised, but luckily they hadn't reached the lockers underneath and stolen anything: if they had we'd have been snookered.

Sometimes, when I look at my passport I can hardly believe I've been to some of the places I have travelled to. While the Tottenham job was hard work, it opened the door to some experiences I would never have otherwise dreamed about. And one journey in particular, a 2003 tour of South Africa, became one of the most memorable trips of my life.

The end-of-season tour in July 2003 saw the club travel to South Africa to support the country's bid for the 2010 World Cup, which, of course, they won. We were due to play matches against Orlando Pirates at the ABSA Stadium in Durban and against Kaiser Chiefs at the Newlands Stadium in Cape Town. It was quite the experience, because we met representatives from the South African 2010 World Cup bid, as well as Archbishop Desmond Tutu and the British High Commissioner. But, for me, it was an excursion to the poverty-stricken townships that would have such a lasting impression.

The first-team squad, the staff and I took time out to visit slums in both cities and held coaching sessions for the underprivileged children. We would arrive by coach on the outskirts of these townships, and a guide explained how these shanty town 'urban living areas' were built on the periphery of towns and cities to house 'non-whites'. Black people were forcibly removed from the towns to live in shacks, and the poverty had become unbearable. But no guide could have prepared us for when we stepped off the coach, and a stream of local children began to pour out of the houses on to a strip of wasteland where we were to hold an impromptu training session.

All the big Spurs players were there – Jamie Redknapp, Robbie Keane, Mauricio Taricco, Helder Postiga and Gustavo Poyet – but, to these forgotten children who had never seen a television set, they were just ordinary men. It was our job to hand out meal tickets, and we were just about to walk in among the kids, offering them around, when the guides called out, 'Don't do that!'

Apparently, we would have been mobbed, such was the poverty. It wasn't anything aggressive, but these kids lived on a hand-to-mouth basis and those meal tickets were like gold dust. We were instructed to hand them out individually, one by one. I remember staring out at all these terrible-looking shacks, cobbled together with sheets of metal and wood. It was horrendous, but, when all these children came scampering towards us where we were waiting with footballs, there was a look in their eyes that I hadn't experienced before or since that day. It was a look that just said, 'Thank you for taking the time to see us, if only for a day, because no one else cares.'

The kids were all ages, and it really made me think about my own daughter, Vikki. The start in life that Vikki had might not have been fantastic, but what I was witnessing made me feel so grateful. Unlike these kids, we had running hot and cold water, and electricity. It made me want to go right into the townships, but our guide said it wasn't recommended, and that it might be dangerous. I remember feeling angry, because I wanted to go in and see exactly what was going on inside these shacks. Everyone from the players to the staff were overawed by the experience, including the club doctor, Mark Curtin, who was really quite emotional.

It turned out that of all the things these kids wanted – not our autographs or our footballs – it was our socks! They just couldn't get them in the townships, and socks were an item of extreme luxury. As the sun dropped behind the shacks on the horizon, all of us removed our socks and handed them out to the children. Even Johnny Wallis, had he been there, would have given these kids a sock without complaint. As our bus drove slowly away from the townships, everyone on board was deathly quiet. Back at our five-star hotel, our squad of superstars walked sombrely and bare-footed across the foyer, without saying a word. And I vowed that one day I would try to return to those townships, and make more of a difference.

CHAPTER 8

THESE COLOURS DON'T RUN

In all my years at Tottenham Hotspur, the biggest controversy to involve the Spurs shirt occurred in 2002, when we won a multi-million-pound sponsorship deal with holiday giant Thomson. It was announced that their logo would replace 'Holsten' on the shirts for the first time in 19 years, which meant that it would be the first time in my career that the shirts would read anything but that famous beer brand. I was looking forward to a change, but it became apparent that some fans were not happy. You see, Thomson's logo was *red*.

'Arsenal shirts are red,' scorned fans, as headlines in the newspapers claimed, 'Spurs fan see red over logo!' The club, and Chairman Daniel Levy, quickly stressed that the sponsorship deal was 'terrific for the fans and the club'. Indeed, Thomson offered the White Hart Lane faithful a discount on their holidays, but, for the purist, the change was an abomination. I couldn't believe it, but, when the news was announced, some fans were coming up to me at the ground and saying, 'How could you let this happen, Roy?' As if the thoughts of the kit man would matter one jot when a company is writing us a cheque for tens of millions of pounds!

Daniel Levy was also quick to point out that for many years red had featured in the official club crest. But where was this red in the club crest? For this, we shall have to take a trip through the history of the Spurs shirt, and its world-famous crest. When I first joined Spurs in 1978, the shirts were very simple lily-white affairs with a handsome blue cockerel on the breast. But soon afterwards, in 1983, when some clothing companies started to rip off our design and flog replica versions, we adapted the crest to feature two heraldic lions and the scroll, reading 'Audere Est Facere' (which, as you probably already know, translates as 'To Dare Is To Do'). And those lions, if you look carefully, are red.

This logo would appear on most of Spurs' playing kits for the next 23 years, and for the rest of my career at the club. So did Spurs fans have anything to complain about? I don't think so; in an era where some Premiership clubs were battling to find a sponsor, I think we should have counted ourselves lucky to have Thomson on board at all. And with the new sponsor came a new kit manufacturer. I had already worked with Admiral shirts, Le Coq Sportif, Hummel, Umbro, Pony and Adidas, but now Italian super-brand Kappa were our kit makers, and they were the first to bring in skin-hugging fabric.

Those Kappa shirts were truly futuristic, and designed to be ultra-stretchy, so, when a player's shirt was being pulled, everyone could see, even those watching at the back of the North Stand. This was good in practice – players like Teddy Sheringham were forever being dragged back by sluggish defenders with no better ideas on how to keep the England International out of their penalty box – but for the fans, particularly those who enjoyed a pint (or ten) after the game, the shirts weren't as forgiving! The club shop was inundated by requests for triple- and quadruple-XL-sized shirts, for our slightly larger fans!

And for those Spurs fans who were complaining about a red sponsor in 2002, they might like to know that Spurs once played in a red strip, although it was many moons ago. It was in 1890, when Spurs moved to a ground on Northumberland Road and supporters queued up to pay 3d (1p) to watch Tottenham Hotspur do battle in what was recorded as 'red shirts and navy shorts'.

Red shirts! This was before we were even a league side, but when Spurs first turned professional in 1896 they celebrated by adopting a new 'chocolate and old gold' strip. (They would later bring this chocolate strip back – for a 2006 Puma away kit that we would use in the UEFA Cup, although I had left the club by then.)

Before 1896, the first records describing Spurs' strip report it as being navy blue. So when exactly did

Tottenham begin to wear those renowned lily-white shirts, and why?

Well, we've been wearing lily-white shirts since 1899, when Spurs moved into White Hart Lane. The white shirt was in homage to Preston North End, who wore white and were at the time the finest team in the land. Most people are surprised to hear that Spurs copied such a lowly team's strip, but you must remember Preston were the number-one team in those days!

But first we wore blue-and-white halved shirts in 1884 after the club had cancelled a fixture to watch Blackburn Rovers play in the English Cup Finals, and were so taken by their blue-and-white halved shirts, we copied them. So Spurs wore Rovers-style outfits from 1884 to 1886. It was a decision that would come back to haunt us 116 years later, when we would face Blackburn in the Worthington Cup Final of 2002.

The game would throw up a kit nightmare that would have given even Johnny Wallis a headache: Spurs had thrashed Chelsea 5–1 at home in one of the most memorable victories in decades. Goals from Iversen, Sherwood, Sheringham, Davies and Rebrov buried our Chelsea hoodoo in superb style and we were to face Blackburn in the final at the Cardiff Millennium Stadium. But Blackburn were drawn as the 'home' team, and would play in their famous blue-and-white-squared home shirts. 2002 was also one of the few seasons where we had elected to not have a yellow away strip. Both of our light- and dark-blue away strips clashed with the opposition, meaning we were officially snookered. There was a lot of head scratching at White Hart Lane, and even the club secretary got involved. The FA was adamant that Blackburn should play in their home kit, so Spurs were left with no other option than to design and manufacture an emergency 'fourth kit'.

It has never been attempted before or after this final, and Adidas later admitted the cost of the process to make just a handful of shirts for the players was akin to that of making 100,000 replica shirts. The golden-yellow Adidas equipment shirts with blue arms were made at great expense, and never to be sold commercially, causing another headache to Spurs' commercial department. If captain Teddy Sheringham lifted the trophy and that picture was beamed to billions of fans worldwide, they'd all want to buy a football shirt that was strictly unavailable. A business nightmare.

I thought I had the solution: in the end we printed up 20 or so white home kits with the names and numbers and Worthington Cup badges, and I kept them in a secret bag with me in the dugout in case we won, and the players would do a quick change. The kit manufacturers weren't the only ones taking victory against Blackburn for granted. In the pubs surrounding the stadium, thousands of Tottenham fans were singing, quite prematurely, 'We're all going on a European tour!' and bookmakers had Tottenham Hotspur odds on favourites to lift the cup.

But Blackburn opened the scoring with a goal from

Matt Jansen in the 25th minute, and the Northern club continued to dominate. Christian Ziege soon equalised for Spurs, but we were clearly not the better team from the offset. A calamitous mistake by Ledley King allowed former Manchester United striker Andrew Cole through on goal, and he tucked the ball away confidently in the 69th minute with a typically instinctive strike. Les Ferdinand could have made the match square after a close one-on-one chance with Friedel, but failed to make anything of it, and in the final minute Teddy Sheringham had a glaringly straightforward penalty appeal turned down by referee Graham Poll: it confirmed that this was not to be our day.

I didn't mind the special golden shirts – they were, in fact, quite fetching. They all had 'Holsten' on them and that was my main concern! But like the Coventry Cup Final where the cock-up saw half the players take to the field without their sponsors, in 2002 it was another example of there being 'something different' about the kit. And, as I've explained before about the peculiarities and superstitions of today's professional footballer, any slight change in routine can sometimes cause a big change on the pitch. While I'm not saying that the colour of the kit could change a result, what I will say is that players take comfort in routine and regularity.

For example, I, like many of the players, didn't like wearing brand-new shorts in any game. Fresh out of the bag, new shorts come up different to washed shorts.

There might be a fault in them that might not have been spotted before. And lo and behold, ten minutes into the Worthington Cup Final, Teddy needed a new pair of shorts because he'd pulled the cord right out of his pair. Often, while players would wear brand-new special shirts for a cup final, the shorts would be the pair they'd worn all season. Throw a special yellow shirt at them and it could make a difference.

Yellow had been Tottenham's away colour of choice since 1969, when Spurs first wore a yellow shirt against Leeds in the league. This was quite a surprise to the Spurs fans, who had been used to seeing us play in dark blue as an away strip for several decades. By way of an explanation, the first programme of the 1969/70 season noted: 'Supporters who travelled to Leeds on Saturday must have been surprised to see the team turn out in yellow shirts with a blue cockerel emblem. As Leeds wear white, we were forced to change. Our change strip in recent years has been navy blue shirts, but this colour has now been banned by the League as it clashes with the referee's outfit.'

Yellow and navy then became Spurs' established alternative colours and remained so for over a decade. When Admiral designed Spurs' new kits in 1977, they took up the theme with a unique shirt with navy-blue epaulettes, a kit I really fancied. But when we played Coventry at home that season, they had a similar Admiral strip, but in brown with yellow epaulettes. I'll never forget seeing them come out of the dressing room, lined up all in brown. It was an absolutely appalling kit!

Over the next few seasons, Spurs became truly established as serious innovators in kit design. For instance, when we signed with French sports manufacturer Le Coq Sportif, who were quite ahead of their time, they introduced the first shadow-striped kits for the team in 1982 to coincide with our centenary year – the type of shiny Polyester shirts that would become emblematic of shirt design of the era. This featured both on the home kit and the powder-blue away kit, together with oversized embroidery, which included '1882–1982'. Le Coq Sportif's name is derived from the Gallic rooster, a national symbol of France, and was obviously a great fit for a club having a cockerel as its icon.

Our cockerel first came along in 1909 when a former player, William James Scott, commissioned a brass casting of a cockerel standing on a football, which was placed high above the West Stand. It was inspired by Harry Hotspur, after whom the club is named and who is reputed to have been a big fan of cock-fighting. Soon afterwards, Spurs played with that cockerel embroidered on to their shirts.

But back to the 1990s, and Spurs were to once again influence modern kit design. When we won our seventh FA Cup in 1991, against Nottingham Forest, we marked the occasion by introducing another innovative strip, this time featuring 'generously cut' shorts. Now, it may not seem outrageous today, but since the 1970s players had worn traditionally short 'budgie-smuggler' shorts, and to have stylish shorts cut just above the knee was quite the head-turner that year.

But some players just couldn't get used to playing in those longer shorts. Some would deliberately order them in two sizes too small. You see, players like Glenn Hoddle used to love really short shorts. In fact, Glenn used to wear the very shortest ones we could find him, and even then he used to roll them up. He would give his three rolls around the waistband before running out. Unbelievable!

Now, I was all for the scientific advancements of sports technology – as long as the shirts kept their shape after a few games, or the shorts didn't fall apart midway through a game. But I wasn't a fan of one of our kit manufacturers' items: the Pony shirts. As kit manager, I had to go around saying how brilliant the new shirts were, to boost sales, but in truth, it was a case of 'Pony by name... Pony by nature'. If you're a cockney, like many Spurs fans are, the word Pony is ingrained in your mind as meaning 'crap', from the rhyming slang 'pony and trap'. It's just not what you want to see emblazoned across players' chests as they run out on to the pitch. You see, to Spurs fans, the shirt is so important and, when you get it wrong, it can really sap moral.

Certain shirts will always remind me of certain players, and certain strips will conjure images of certain goals, or moments. Some are obvious: if you show me a 1989 Hummel home shirt, with the blue chevrons down the sleeves, I'll think of Gary Lineker. But show me a 1987

Hummel with the blue pattern on the chest, and I'll think of Nico Claesen, for some completely unaccountable reason. The 1995 Pony home shirt reminds me of Chris Armstrong and a fantastic North London derby in which he scored.

Before I started working for Spurs, when I was just a fan, I used to absolutely love the 1967 strip. It was the perfect Tottenham kit: a plain white shirt with a bold cockerel and no shield on the breast, with plain blue shorts and white socks. That to me, is Tottenham Hotspur, and reminds me of Jimmy Greaves. Throw a pair of white shorts on to that, and you've got Spurs' European glories; in this outfit, anything was possible and, on this uniform, the colours don't run.

I loved it when we went back to wearing all white, because it would remind me of when I used to watch European games at White Hart Lane when I was a kid. I always thought the home shirts should be as close to unadulterated white as possible, although when Hummel produced a white shirt and white shorts for the league in 1985, I remember feeling put out that, by playing in all white in the league, it would take the shine off wearing an all-white outfit in Europe. I'm a purist at heart, you see, and it was nothing to do with the fact that it was hard to get the mud stains out of white shorts – honestly!

I was always more inclined towards simpler shirt designs, and, although I'd get asked my opinion at the design stage, at the end of the day it was all about sales. Fans used to knock yellow as an away kit, but it sold well and I used to like it from a professional point of view because it didn't clash with anything. Pale-blue shirts used to worry me, because, with a low sun, that kit used to look white over the far side of the pitch. And apart from playing Fulham, who else would you wear a dark-blue shirt against? If you play Sheffield Wednesday or Blackburn, what do you wear then? That's why I loved yellow. I always admired Adidas shirts, simply for the quality of the product, and Umbro were also fantastic. Umbro was one of the best all-round kits we ever had, and it was brilliant, from the training socks all the way up to match kit.

I only wish I'd kept some of it, but, like Johnny Wallis before me, my view was that the kit always seemed such a disposable commodity. The first-team shirts would be handed down to the reserve team, and then to the Academy, who eventually would use the rags to clean the boots and even the toilets. As I said, I never had any interest in collecting – when I got home the last thing I wanted to look at was another bloody Spurs shirt!

A few of the players took an interest in the kit, and would either keep hold of their match shirt or swap it with an opponent. Robbie Keane went through a phase of collecting and swapping shirts during the Kappa years but it became an expensive habit. The lads would be given two home shirts and two away, and, if they used any more than that, they'd be charged for them! It sounds tight, but we had a budget, and one year I worked out that they'd thrown £8000 worth of shirts into the crowd, or swapped them with the opposition. So I'd collect all the shirts in at the end of the game, much like a Sunday-league manager would, and make a list of who had swapped theirs or thrown it in the crowd. Those whose shirts were missing would be marked on the team sheet as 'GOK', which meant 'Gift Of Kit', and the cost of the shirt would be taken out of their wage packet.

That said, I was lucky enough to have been given a handful of shirts by some of the players I was very close to. I was very proud when Ledley King handed me one of his England shirts, after he made the first team to play Austria in September 2004. I suppose all those old shirts I handled over the years would be worth a fortune nowadays, but who could have predicted that 30 years ago? Memorabilia experts would weep into their sales catalogues if they knew what happened to most of those original shirts, but, if it's any consolation, I thought they made excellent mops to clean my kit-room floor!

The shirts belonged to the club and my job was simply to make the players' lives easier. It could be hard looking after some players, and I often had the sense that some players would never be happy, no matter how clean their shirt or how perfect the fit. I remember Mido was one of those players. He was a good player, and I liked him as a man, but whatever I gave him was either too big, or too small or just 'wrong'! One time he was begging me for another pair of socks, and I was about to tell him to sling his hook, when I suddenly realised, 'My God, I've turned into Johnny Wallis!'

Johnny told me, all those years ago, 'You're more than a kit man, you're an agony aunt.' Because if a player has a grievance, it might cause a row if he tells the boss, and if he goes to the assistant manager he might tell the Gaffa anyway. But tell the kit man and it goes no further. I've had generations of Spurs legends in my little office moaning their heads off. Most of the time, I couldn't tell you what they said! I'd have Ginola in there, saying, 'Sacre bleu! He is a wanker! I cannot play with him one second longer!' and I'd say, 'Yeah, you're right, David.' And I didn't even know who he was talking about! If those walls had ears... but luckily it was just me and 2,000 pairs of socks.

When George Graham became Spurs manager in October 1998, he asked me on his very first day, 'How could your job be made easier?'

I told him, 'It makes sense to have the laundry at the training ground.'

You can say what you like about George Graham, but he made it happen just like that: they built me a laundry on to the back of the building. I soon had my own kit room, my own office and a storeroom. They installed gas, electricity and water, the works – and I loved it. That place really changed my job, because then I was always on site and there wasn't any needless delivering kit across North London in the van. But best of all, I had a little area to call my own, and it quickly became a bit of a sanctuary for the players. In fact, I used to say that they gained entry into my 'inner sanctum'. It was an area where the players could chill out and have a laugh and a joke out of sight of the physio or the manager.

Paul Robinson used to be a regular visitor. He'd pop in and say hello to the girls in the laundry, then come into my room and read the papers. Freddie Kanoute came in one day, and he said, 'Roy, it's Ramadan, I need to pray. Have you got any towels?'

And so I let him into my back office and he knelt down on my towel to pray. I'd never seen a Muslim pray before, and Fred explained, 'I'm praying to Mecca.'

'That's funny,' I joked, 'I didn't even know you liked bingo!' But it went right over his head.

Under George Graham, the training facilities became excellent. There was a proper boot room and individual lockers, and the players used to bend balls around wooden defensive walls painted to look like Spurs legends like Jürgen Klinsmann. By this time in my career, being first-team kit man became more than a job, it became a way of life. Kit men from visiting teams would come by before a game, and we'd have a chat before kick-off. Sometimes they'd say, 'I forgot my slips, or vests,' and you would help each other out.

People are always surprised to hear that I have a great relationship with Vic Akers, my opposite number at Arsenal. He went on to manage Arsenal Ladies to two championship titles, and Vic served as long at Arsenal as I did at Spurs. We had a fantastic relationship, because we had a lot in common. Yes, there was a rivalry there, and I wanted to beat Arsenal as much as the next man, but, if ever Vic wanted anything, I'd give it to him. Over the seasons I got close to most of the other kit men in the Premiership, who proved I wasn't the only slightly mad one.

There was a kit manager called Pudsey, at Fulham, and to this day I don't know his real name. We just knew that he was also the fella in the Pudsey Bear outfit on *Comic Relief*, and that he loved Country and Western music. I'd often find Pudsey at Craven Cottage's gym, pedalling away on an exercise bike in a pair of cowboy boots and hat, singing along to loud Country and Western tunes. I did tell you, us kit managers are all a little crazy. And we like to keep it in the family too. I got my nephew, Gary Gray, a job at Fulham with Pudsey for five years, and, when Pudsey left, he took over. Fulham were with Adidas at the time and so were Spurs, and we had a great relationship with the German manufacturer. One day they sent us all a present of Adidas predator boots with our names embroidered on: 'Pudsey', 'Roysie' and 'Mini-me', my nephew. Gary is now the kit man at Chelsea and occasionally he rings me up and asks me questions, just like I used to ask Johnny.

I'd had a wealth of experience and I was always happy to share. I'm into my carp fishing, and often I'll see a bloke on the riverbank and ask, 'Caught anything today?' and he'll say, 'Nothing,' lying through his teeth!

If I know something that can help, I'll tell someone, even if they are the Chelsea or even Arsenal kit man, for the reason that, if I were a hundred miles from home, I'd hope they'd do the same for me. Because in today's game, you can forget one key item of equipment and the whole team can fall apart.

Take Edgar Davids, who signed for Spurs in 2005. He was great company, Edgar, but hard work. He kept every single shirt I ever game him, giving them away to family and friends, often two shirts a game whether he played or not. But he also had glaucoma and had to wear custom-made Nike glasses. It was an added bit of stress, because, if you forgot those bloody glasses, the Dutch International couldn't play. What's more he later started to colour coordinate them with the kits, and had a yellow pair specially made for the away kit. It was a nightmare, in truth, but it had to be done. But I used to wonder what Johnny Wallis would have made of today's footballers.

I'd often think of Johnny Wallis, years after he had departed the club. You see, by my following him, just two men had looked after those famous lily-white shirts for half a century, and we took the job incredibly seriously. Tottenham Hotspur was Johnny's life, until 2003, when he sadly passed away on 25 February at the North Middlesex Hospital, Edmonton, just yards from White Hart Lane. I will always remember him fondly.

CHAPTER 9

MANAGERS, MANAGERS, MANAGERS

I worked under an astonishing 17 managers and first-team coaches during my time at Tottenham Hotspur – one Irishman, one Scotsman, a Frenchman, one Dutch, one Swiss, ten Englishman, one World Cup winner, and David Pleat a record four times. David had more comebacks than Elton John, and I was there for each of his stints in the big chair, including three as caretaker manager.

When I first started, Keith Burkinshaw was in charge – a dour Yorkshireman who was always very blunt and to the point. Keith had played just one game for Liverpool in his seven years at the club, but in December 1957 he left for Workington Town, where he carved out a career, making 293 league appearances and scoring nine goals before leaving for Scunthorpe United in May 1965. Keith was a coach at Newcastle United from 1968 until 1975, when he was sacked as part of a cost-cutting exercise, and it was then that Spurs manager Terry Neill hired him as first-team coach. In the summer of 1976, Neill resigned to become manager of Arsenal, and the unassuming Burkinshaw was appointed as his replacement.

Keith was a fine coach with a fantastic sense of humour. I remember the time when I was working on the ground staff, tending to the lush green playing surface at White Hart Lane with groundsman Colin White. Keith had this funny sway of a walk, and, when I saw him approaching, I tapped Colin and said, 'Here we go!'

Keith said, 'Aye up' – his typical Yorkshire greeting – and Colin and I stood up with our pitchforks in our hands.

'How's the pitch, son?' Keith asked.

'Yeah, all right, Gaffa, why?' Colin replied.

'I can see lots of indentations,' said the Yorkshireman, and the way he said the word reduced us to laughter.

'Don't you mean holes, Keith?' we laughed.

And he said, 'No! Indentations.'

The word would become a catchphrase for years to come. Keith was always such fun, and was so laidback. He used to confide a lot in Steve Perryman as his captain, and Steve would make all the decisions on Keith's behalf out on the pitch. It was an almost telepathic relationship they had, and so Keith was never very vocal in the dugout. A bit like Bill Nicholson before him: all his work was done Monday to Friday on the training pitch and he would sit back and enjoy Saturdays.

Keith was always involved in the practical jokes at

Spurs, and often the butt of them too, but he took it all very well. He could take a joke as well as he could dish it out. Once, when the team went to Japan on tour, the lads played a trick on Keith at a restaurant meal that had been organised for the team. Making sure the Gaffa went in first, they said to him, 'It's Japan, Keith, and it's tradition for you to take your shoes off.'

Well, Keith took off his shoes and left them outside, and so did all the players. But, as they walked through, the players slipped their shoes back on, and Keith was met by an apologetic Japanese maitre d', who bowed and said to him, 'Sir, you do not have to remove your shoes, it is not that kind of restaurant.'

Keith turned to the players and said in his trademark Yorkshire accent, 'Right, it's OK, lads, you can put…' But, of course, they were all stood there already wearing their shoes and a smirk.

In another restaurant, Keith had put his coat on the back of his chair, and every time the lads walked past him, they'd slip a knife or a fork into his pocket! Then one of the team quietly took the waiter aside and said, 'I don't want to alarm you, but that Yorkshireman in the corner is stealing cutlery.' Well, the waiter approached Keith who, protesting his innocence, held up his jacket to prove it – and it sounded like 'Tubular Bells'!

He was always great fun, was Keith, and he gave me my big break at Spurs and for that I loved him, but he would come to experience some real ups and downs, weathering the storm of relegation in 1977 and gaining promotion the year after. He signed Ossie Ardiles and Ricky Villa, won the FA Cup twice and won the UEFA Cup on penalties, making him the second most successful manager in Tottenham's history. Replacing him was going to be hard.

Peter Shreeves, Keith's assistant, took over in June 1984 and if you ask anyone at Tottenham they'll tell you he was a top coach. Peter was always out on the training field taking sessions, and as a London lad he shared a sense of humour with the squad. Oh, and he could play a bit, too. Peter used to turn out in those infamous five-a-side games on a Monday evening and one night, after he scored a particularly tasty goal, he ran up to me and said, 'Roy, Roy! Stop the game!' I picked up the ball and he said, 'Call the fire brigade!'

I suddenly felt concerned, and I asked, 'Why, Pete? What's the matter?'

He just laughed. 'My left foot is on fire tonight, son!'

He also used to say to me in those five-a-side games, 'Give it to me, I've got a plan.' Just like on *The A-Team*, the TV programme that had just become popular at the time. And boy did he have a plan. Shreeves took Spurs directly to third place in the league at the end of his first season as manager. This would normally have earned them a UEFA Cup place, but the ban on English clubs in European competitions began at this time – due to the Heysel Stadium disaster – which was bitterly disappointing.

Peter was always immaculately dressed. He was the

only coach who would iron creases in his tracksuit! He'd wear a posh dogtooth jacket with matching hanky and tie. My groundsman pal Colin White used to do a mean impression of Shreeves' voice, which he had down to a fine art. Colin would hide round corners and call players' names, and even Shreeves used to find it funny. But Tottenham finished tenth the following season and Shreeves was sacked in favour of David Pleat in March 1986.

David Pleat had a football brain like no other managers. He brought Mitchell Thomas along with him from Luton, and among his earliest changes at the club would be the signing of Nico Claesen and Richard Gough. During his time as manager, Tottenham Hotspur attained third place in the First Division and reached the FA Cup Final and the semi-final of the Football League Cup in the 1986/87 season. He had some funny ways about him, did David Pleat, but I thought he was tremendous for the club.

However, I had a difference of opinion with his assistant, Trevor Hartley, once. It was right in the middle of the deep freeze of 1987, when a record 65cm of snow fell on the south of England and the country experienced sustained freezing temperatures. To say it was a bit parky was an understatement! Undershirts are the norm nowadays and most players wear something under their shirt today, but back then it was unheard of. I spoke to Johnny Wallis and said, 'We've got to get the lads some vests, this chill is unbearable.'

I suggested that I get in touch with a local shop and buy a bulk order of thermal vests, and David Pleat agreed, but told me to speak to Trevor to get the money for 75 vests, 'for the first team, reserves and the apprentices'.

Trevor said, 'It's a good idea, but do we need them for the reserves? Why don't we buy them just for the first team?'

I said, 'Look, the reserves will get just as cold as the first team, we're all playing in the same weather.'

But Trevor wasn't having it. 'Yeah, but it'll be a good incentive for them to make it into the first team.'

Well, I didn't agree with that at all. I couldn't see how a thermal vest could ever be the incentive for a player to make the first team. What about the glory of playing for Spurs? And anyway, if one man was going to be warm that winter, they should all be warm. I ended up going back to Pleat, and he agreed. It was a sticky situation though, I'd only been in the job five minutes and I was arguing with the assistant manager. We got the vests in the end. I knew we all had the team's best interest at heart, so once we'd sorted it out there wasn't any bad blood or anything. As it happens David Pleat left the club soon after, but by no means would this be the last time I would work with the man.

You see, whenever you're the new manager, you're the fruit of the day. There's a honeymoon period, but it always takes a bit of settling in. And when results don't go your way, sometimes at Spurs more so than at other clubs, you can quickly fall foul of the fans and the board. So, when David moved on, we had an interim period with Trevor and Doug Livermore, and there was intense speculation about who was coming in next. Then the name Terry Venables came up.

Venables had been captain of Chelsea and won the League Cup in 1965, scoring in the final against Leicester City. He had made 202 appearances for Chelsea and scored 26 goals before being sold to Tottenham Hotspur for £80,000 in 1966. He played 115 league games and scored 19 goals for Spurs, with the highlight being an FA Cup Final win over his old side, giving him all the credentials to be a very exciting prospect as a Spurs manager. And a cockney boy, too!

When he arrived, he brought with him Alan Harris, who he'd been with at QPR. Terry had buckets of charisma about him – he was one of those men with an aura. And the players he attracted... well, he bought Paul Gascoigne from the nose of Alex Ferguson, which, as I've mentioned, was one of the steals of the century.

Now, some managers I've worked with got involved with everything, from the first team to the football shirts. Many wanted to know the ins and outs, others just let you get on with it. Terry Venables was a bit of both. Providing things were running smoothly, he let you get on with it, but he was quite passionate about the new strips. All managers look at the new kits as they come in, and, as kit manager, you'll meet with the commercial director and the club secretary, and work with the kit company to narrow down their designs to two or three. Then the chairman takes over, and they decide the next year's kit. I remember Terry was very vocal in deciding our posh Umbro home shirts, making sure we had an appropriately smart uniform to match our exciting new style.

But Terry's real talent was in the dugout. There were the times when games weren't going our way, and you'd think, 'There's no way out of this,' and of course at that point there's 30,000 football managers in the stadium. But all of a sudden Terry would make one or two changes – not even a substitution – and he would change our luck. To have that ability to transform a game just from the sidelines is amazing. Most managers will make a tactical decision by changing a player, but Terry could shuffle the pack and the whole game of cards would change.

Terry was also by far the most entertaining manager I ever shared a bench with. He and Alan Harris were like a double act. Terry would be cracking jokes, and, when the crowd were having a go at him, he'd just turn and give this look over his shoulder that said: 'Don't start!' And if someone shouted something at him, Terry would turn around and nail him, all in one put-down line. I lost count of the times I saw a supporter shuffle up the stairs in embarrassment after experiencing the sharp tongue of Terry Venables. On the other hand, he was immensely popular with the staff because he cared. For instance, the club would organise a Christmas party, but Terry would also put on his own private do, and they were always great fun.

In the FA Cup-winning year of 1991, Venables became chief executive of Tottenham Hotspur, and Peter Shreeves would again take charge of first-team duties. Venables joined forces with businessman Sir Alan Sugar to take over Tottenham Hotspur PLC and pay off its £20 million debt, part of which involved the sale of Gascoigne, much to everyone's sadness. But Shreeves' second spell as team manager lasted just one season before he was dismissed in favour of joint coaches Ray Clemence and Doug Livermore. They were like 'good cop, bad cop'. Clem was very fiery as a player, and as a manager he was even more so. Dougie was the manager and Clem was his assistant, and, while Dougie was tactical and would be trying to calm the team down, Clem would come in like an explosion, winding them all up! It was always going to be an interim period, and I suspect Doug wouldn't have taken the job anyway. As individuals, the players had utmost respect for both of those men, and I think they both realised how tough being a manager to 20 professional footballers was, with all those egos and the psychologies.

Even in my capacity, I'd have to learn how each player reacted. You get to know the ones to whom you could say, 'That's not you today, mate, what's going on? You're better than that.' Other players would go into their shell, and others would bite your head off if you dared say something. Take my relationship with a player and multiply it by a thousand, and that's a manager. A manager needs to know the difference between a Gazza –

who needed an arm round the shoulder – and another type of player who needed a kick up the arse. In a managerial capacity, you need so many different acts to get your players working.

Tottenham's first Premier League season ended with a mid-table finish and Venables was removed from the club's board after a legal dispute with Sir Alan that went to the High Court. Everyone was relieved when Ossie Ardiles became the club's next manager in 1993. Under Ardiles, Tottenham employed the 'Famous Five': Teddy Sheringham and Jürgen Klinsmann up front, Nick Barmby just behind, Darren Anderton on the right and Ilie Dumitrescu on the left. Klinsmann was a sensation, scoring remarkable goals and becoming a firm favourite with his self-deprecating 'dive celebration'.

But these expensive foreign signings made little difference to Tottenham's form, as, during the 1994 close season, the club was found guilty of making illegal payments to players and given one of the most severe punishments in English football history: a 12-point deduction, a one-year FA Cup ban and a £600,000 fine. Luckily, Sir Alan stepped in and the cup ban and points deduction were quashed. Ossie had a lot of work to do.

But, mercifully, he had Stevie Perryman as his number two, and Stevie was very much the operational side of things: Ossie was the philosophy, but Perryman put it into practice. Spurs have always been a traditional footballing team, and we always try to play the right way. We've never smashed it up-field. But Ossie was massively into passing and attractive football. He used to say in his strong accent, 'Play, play, play, play, play!' His accent hadn't changed, despite over a decade of playing and managing English-speaking teams in both England and America. But who would change that for the world, as Spurs fans still sing 'In the Cup for Tottingham' on the terraces!

Stevie used to pull his hair out, as he was a defender at heart and Ossie was an out-and-out attacker. With Ossie it was like the old cavalier charge, but Stevie was concerned with the leaking holes in the defence, and was always trying to plug the holes that our attackers left in the back. Ossie would just say, 'Play, play, play, play!' While there was definitely a conflict there, Perryman and Ardiles had won cups together and travelled the world together and were very close. We were always going to win 5–4 or lose 5–4, on any given Saturday. You'd be 3–0 up at White Hart Lane and be thinking, 'If we're lucky, we could scrape a draw here!' It was heart-in-your-mouth stuff, every match. It was all or nothing.

Ossie was holding a typical team meeting one afternoon, saying as usual, 'Play, play, play,' when Colin Calderwood, our centre half and a dry Scotsman, put his hand up and said, 'Gaffa, you keep talking about the fab five, but what about the shit six?'

Everyone fell about laughing. But he was right. There were big problems at the back.

There was also an occasion at a reserve match, when I

was stood on the line with reserves manager Pat Holland (the former West Ham player), Ossie Ardiles and the rest of the Spurs staff. Suddenly, Ossie yelled, 'Pat! Tunny Fizz!' and everyone looked at each other. 'Tunny Fizz!' yelled Ossie again, and no one knew what he was on about. Everyone started moving away because it was embarrassing! We were thinking, 'What is this "Tunny Fizz"? – "Turn and face?"' It transpired that Ossie was calling for 'Tony, the physio', but it took five minutes to figure it out!

I loved Ossie, and, having been on the ground staff when he signed in 1978, it was great for me to work with him in a professional capacity on his second stint at the club. To me he was a marvel as a footballer: he was just ten stone, dripping wet, but I don't remember him getting knocked off the ball once. He had this uncanny ability to dribble with the ball with his toes, like a ballet dancer. And he would drop a shoulder so convincingly that he wouldn't just beat a player, he'd turn them inside out. As a manager, you couldn't say he didn't entertain the crowd... although not always in the right way. It was exciting, but I knew we couldn't play that brand of football forever, and finally Ardiles was sacked in September 1994.

Stevie Perryman took over as interim manager, and then Gerry Francis turned up. Francis initially turned around the club's fortunes dramatically, as we quickly climbed to seventh in the league and reached the FA Cup semi-finals, a cup we were lucky to be playing in after the FA case, but we lost 4–1 to eventual winners Everton. I really fancied us but we got beaten, in typical fashion at the time, by giving away soft goals at the back. The result really hurt.

I'll never forget that game because my daughter Vikki and my wife went along with all the players' wives. There was a posh coach leaving from White Hart Lane and they took the journey up there with the partners of Teddy Sheringham, Nicky Barmby and the rest of the team. It was a real treat, but Vikki tells the story about when they arrived at Everton and one drunken fan noticed the Spurs logo on the coach and assumed the bus contained the players behind the darkened windows. Anyway, this guy was throwing abuse at the bus, flicking his fingers, when Vikki noticed that in his excitement the man's wallet had fallen out of his pocket. Well, all the wives and girlfriends were trying to tell him, pointing at the wallet and waving to him, but this idiot thought they were giving him stick back. So, as the bus took off, the drunk sprinted after the bus and all the girls got really frightened that he'd catch up with it. But luckily he didn't, and the drunk was intercepted by a challenge from a particularly tough tackling lamp-post, into which he ran head-first! I wish I'd seen it.

Gerry Francis was a fine player in his day, and I believe that he had children later in life, and was very family orientated. Gerry always made sure staff and players got the right amount of time off with their families, probably because he felt he needed it himself. I loved working for Gerry, and I remember one Tuesday afternoon at the training ground he called a meeting and said, 'I want all the staff to have a day off tomorrow, and that means everyone.'

The whole place was buzzing with excitement, but I had far too much to do. So I thought I'd sneak in at half past six the next morning, sort the kit out, and then leave at ten. But when I arrived at my kit room, Gerry Francis followed me in and said, 'What are you doing here?' I told him I had a lot on, but he was insistent. He told me to go home immediately and spend some time with my family, and even waited for me to lock the door and leave. He was a very thoughtful manager.

We had some great footballing times under Gerry, too. As an attacking midfield player himself, he gave our midfield a free reign, and it worked. He also signed David Ginola from Newcastle United to add a foreign flavour to our midfield and some excitement to the Spurs team. David became a firm favourite at White Hart Lane and, although he wasn't fully fit – and it took time for him to lose some weight and get match fit – his performances brought such flair to the games and so many spectacular goals.

But mid-table finishes in the next two seasons were unconvincing and Francis resigned in November 1997, with Spurs battling against relegation from the Premier League. Nine times out of ten it's the results that cause a manager to go. The crowd get on your back, and then you've had it. Some managers you never saw again... the likes of Santini and Gross, they just melted into history, but, like Terry before him, Gerry went round every member of staff the day he left, shook hands and thanked us for all the help we'd given him. He was a real gentleman to the very end, and a lot of today's managers could learn a lot from him.

Chris Hughton – who, like Steve Perryman, was 'Mr Tottenham' – took over for the next interim. At the time Chris and I had been at the club for the longest out of all the staff, so I enjoyed his brief tenure. I'd never heard of Christian Gross, when he eventually took over, but I will talk more of him later. After Gross came George Graham, a particularly controversial choice due to his previous association with Arsenal, but in his first season as Spurs manager the club secured a mid-table finish and won the League Cup. In the final against Leicester City at Wembley, fullback Justin Edinburgh was sent off after trading blows with Robbie Savage, but Spurs secured a dramatic victory through Allan Nielsen's diving header in the 93rd minute of the game.

Spurs also reached the semi-finals of the FA Cup, where we were beaten 2–0 by Newcastle after extra time, and, to cap a good season, star player David Ginola won both the PFA Players' Player of the Year 1999 award and Football Writers' Association Footballer of the Year 1999 award.

Of course, we knew George Graham as a manager

from the amazing success he had at Arsenal, and I always thought he was on a hiding to nothing simply because he'd been at 'that club down the road'. The true Spurs fan can't stand anything about that red-and-white mob from Highbury.

But, speaking as an employee, I thought George Graham was brilliant. He demanded and got the utmost respect – from the office staff to the players and coaches. We all called him 'Mr Graham', or 'Gaffa', or 'Boss'. That was just how it was. No one called him George. However, he could never get Tottenham above tenth in the Premiership, and he was sacked as manager in March 2001 after falling out with the club's new chairman, Daniel Levy. Looking this time for a manager who was a Spurs legend, and not an Arsenal one, the position was filled by a former Spurs player whose pedigree could not be argued.

Glenn Hoddle took over in April 2001, with the team lying stagnant and 13th in the table. His first game saw defeat to Arsenal in an FA Cup semi-final, but Hoddle turned for inspiration to more experienced players in the shape of Teddy Sheringham, Gus Poyet and Christian Ziege, and Spurs' entire football outlook changed within months of his appointment. The season of 2001/02 saw Spurs finish in ninth place, as well as reaching the League Cup Final, where we lost to Blackburn Rovers, having destroyed Chelsea 5–1 in the previous round. One of the biggest things with Glenn was that, at 44 years of age, he'd join in with training and he'd be just as good – if not better – than the players he was coaching. Of course, he couldn't run about like he used to, but when he joined in training sessions he'd still boss it.

At staff games at the end of the season, we'd play a match against the Academy, and we had a hell of a team – Stevie Perryman, Hoddle, John Gorman, Hans Segers – and Hoddle was out of this world. Of course, we'd cheat like hell, and we'd never let the kids beat us even if we had to play on till it was dark.

Back in the Premiership, Hoddle was named Premiership Manager of the Month for August 2002 after Spurs ended the month top of the league. But we inevitably slipped to tenth, and the pressure began to build on Hoddle, and he was finally sacked in September 2003 after a poor start to the season, in which the team picked up just four points from their opening six league games.

In May 2004, Tottenham signed French team manager Jacques Santini as head coach, with Martin Jol as his assistant and Frank Arnesen as sporting director. I certainly knew nothing of Santini, other than that he spoke no English. To simply ask him what kit he wanted to wear for training was an impossibility. But I found myself working directly with Martin Jol, who spoke perfect English and with whom I would strike up a good relationship.

I found Santini very strange; he rarely spoke in the

dressing room. There'd be this silence and you'd be expecting him to say something… but nothing. It was certainly different. When Santini quit the club in bizarre circumstances after just 13 games, Martin became the number one, and I was quite relieved. Jol was a great man-manager and knew when to administer a cuddle and when to let off fireworks. He had loads of new ideas when it came to training, and involved Chrissie Hughton a lot in his work. The lads really enjoyed playing under him, because he played a decent style of football.

The big Dutchman became a favourite with the passionate Spurs crowd and secured a ninth-place finish. In the 2005/06 campaign, his first full season, and my last, he almost managed to secure a Champions League place. But Spurs missed out on the final day of the season, and, like everything involved with the club's history thus far, nothing would be simple. But I will talk more of that later. For now, I'd like to take you inside the dressing room and reveal the innermost secrets of some of the Premiership's most superstitious footballers.

CHAPTER 10
SUPERSTITIONS OF THE STARS

Many of Tottenham Hotspur's greatest footballers (and some of our worst) were the most superstitious young men I have ever encountered. As kit manager, I came to learn the intricate details of each of their obsessive and compulsive habits that occupied them before a game. From the international player who insisted on walking round half-naked before kick-off, to the midfielder who once took a pair of scissors to his own shirt, I'm going to reveal for the first time the unique traits that some of Spurs' finest *must* do in the dressing room before taking to the field.

Goalkeepers are, by their very nature, nutty, and they're often the most meticulous and superstitious members of the squad. A lot can go wrong for a keeper and, when it does, it's always a disaster, so it's understandable they're incredibly superstitious. 'Never mess with a goalkeeper's gloves' – that's what I learned.

Some win a game or keep a clean sheet and throw the gloves away, but for others those gloves become sacred 'winning gloves' and they'll wear them till they lose. Get it wrong and throw away a pair of winning gloves, and there's big trouble. Just ask Paul Robinson, one of the few goalkeepers to have scored a goal for Tottenham Hotspur, along with Pat Jennings. When Robbo first signed for Spurs, he would wear a pair for a game and if he won, or if they 'felt right', I'd wash them by hand and keep them special for him, with the match kit.

Robbo would take up to four pairs to a game, but I'd be looking after his special gloves like they were the crown jewels. It can sometimes be a nightmare for sponsors, because they like to see their sponsees wearing brand-new gloves, and, when a goalkeeper has a winning streak, they can be seen wearing knackered gloves. I remember with Erik Thorstvedt, if he liked a pair of gloves, he'd wear them right out. I think his sponsors were tearing their hair out, as they'd be falling off his hands at the end. I bet they were praying for him to let in a few so he'd wear a new pair! He was such a big guy, Erik. He caused our shirt sponsors a few headaches too. We had our manufacturers make a special shirt for him, because his upper body was so long. Washing them felt like washing a pair of curtains.

Other players, such as Pat Van Den Hauwe, would take matters into their own hands. I used to get along great guns with Pat: he was like an original tough guy, and was a fine pro. But he revealed his personal superstition the first time he was playing in the reserves. We used to only pack long-sleeved shirts in the winter: while the first team used to get a choice, in the reserves it was long-sleeved or nothing. Anyway, Pat was different, and come rain or shine or 100 degrees below he'd wear short sleeves, and that day he got to the reserves game, he said, 'Short-sleeved, please.' And I said, 'We haven't got one, Pat.'

He was clearly upset; I could see it straight away. I thought maybe it was partly that he was suffering the indignity of playing for the reserves, but in fact he was just awfully superstitious and would only wear short-sleeved shirts. Later, the team ran out on to the pitch, and someone poked me and said, 'Who's Fred Flintstone out there?' I looked out on to the field, and there was Pat, happily playing in short sleeves, having taken scissors to the sleeves... rather messily. He looked like Captain Caveman!

Stephen Carr was superstitious about his sleeves, too. He'd wear long sleeves in the first half and short sleeves in the second half, week in, week out. I've seen it happen: a player has a great game and they'll look back and see what they did 'right'. They'll try to replicate that luck by keeping things the same. Stephen had changed shirts at half-time once, played well, and probably will never alter his routine till he stops playing. As a kit man, it's my job to respect these mad little traits and superstitions, because, if a player isn't happy, he won't play well.

If someone put a shirt on and it didn't feel right, I'd

change it and humour them, even if I knew that if I gave them another shirt it would be exactly the same size and fit: they're identical! But it's a nervous thing. Certain players would only wear a certain pair of shorts. They'd say, 'These feel really good,' and I'd write their initials in the label. Gazza was like that. We were playing Manchester United at home, and it was five minutes before kick-off and everyone was rushing around, when Gazza collared me and said, 'Roysie, these shorts don't feel right.'

I'd put his initials on the shorts so I knew they were the ones he'd been wearing all season. The boys were just about to run out so I was under immense pressure... I had to do something quick. So I went behind the dressing-room door, shook the shorts and folded them up, then I came back in and said, 'There you go, Gazza, brand new.' He looked at them, put them on and said, 'Cheers, Roy, that's much better.' They were the same pair.

Other players had some quite bizarre habits when it came to their boots. Some players wore new boots every game, while others were so superstitious they'd keep the same ones for weeks. Some trained in the match boots, and others had a special match pair. But when Romanian player Ilie Dumitrescu started at the club, he did something that surprised even me. He came up to me just before his debut and said, 'Would you mind cutting the feet off my socks?'

I didn't have time to argue, so I did it. As I quickly

learned, Dumitrescu used to order his boots half a size too small, tore out the inner sole, and he played in them *barefoot*. He'd put his foot straight in the boot, and he'd tie the boot as tight as he could. Then he'd soak them in water, so the boots were absolutely skin-tight. He used to say, 'It's so I can feel the ball.' It was crazy! But it worked for him.

It certainly caught on, and many players, including David Ginola, started to cut the feet off their socks, and wore a thin cotton sock and taped the two together. If you ever walk around the dressing room while the match is on, you'll see several lonely 'feet-bits' of sock lying around.

Gary Mabbutt would turn each shinpad round six revolutions before it went into the sock. He'd count them: one, two, three, four, five, six... and into the sock! Again, bizarre, but it worked for him. Other players, especially in the old days, didn't like to wear shinpads at all, and until 1990 it wasn't compulsory. Tony Galvin never wore a shinpad. One time he came into the dressing room at half-time with his shins hacked to pieces. I said, 'Tony, you've got to wear protection.' He agreed and rolled on a tubigrip bandage under his sock... and ran out again. Unbelievable!

'Shinpads restrict my running, Roysie,' Gary Lineker told me one afternoon, after I insisted he wore protection. 'So does a broken leg,' I told him. But he'd still not bother with shinpads.

Years later, Robbie Keane would be the same, but by

that time wearing pads was required by FA regulations. So, one afternoon, on Robbie's demands I took my trusty hacksaw to the smallest plastic shinpad I could find and managed to whittle it down to a tiny strip barely the size of a cigarette packet. 'Thanks, Roysie,' he said, slipping the pathetic piece of plastic into his sock. 'They want me to wear shinpads, I'll wear shinpads.

Kasey Keller, on the other hand, would wear pads so big he could have opened the batting for England! Goalkeepers – who'd be one?

When Ray Clemence was in goal for Spurs, he had one of the more interesting pre-match routines. Ray liked to be the first at the ground and would turn up hours before everyone else. He'd get his ankles strapped, put his slip on and walk around for ages like that, essentially in his pants. He'd be in the dressing room moving round doing all kinds of stretches, all in a particular order... just in his slip! It was remarkable to see the intricacies of this man's routine, although it was lucky there were no ladies present!

Klinsmann was never very superstitious, although he was certainly eccentric and used to turn heads at the training ground when he arrived in his VW Beetle. None of the other players could understand it – they were all fighting to have the latest BMW or Mercedes, and Jürgen would pootle to training in this knackered heap. But who could argue, when he was such an amazing player. I remember his debut at Sheffield Wednesday: everyone in the dressing room was talking about what Jürgen should do if he scored, because he was getting all kinds of stick for allegedly being a bit of a diver. They had it all planned before and, when he scored that header and did his now famous dive celebration, it was one of the best things I ever saw at Spurs.

Jürgen was fantastic to work with. He'd ask me to whiten the stripes of the Reebok logo on his boots: he knew how to play the sponsorship game. But I remember one time when I arrived in the first-team dressing room to hear the German unleashing a terrible tirade... he was furious! It turned out he was unhappy after the warm-up, having discovered we were practising with plain white Mitre balls, whereas we used special Premier League balls during the match. I'd never seen him lose his temper before, but he'd come in spitting feathers! 'I want to warm up with the proper ball!' he was yelling. You see, we normally take four or five match balls, so I quickly gave them all to him.

I did wonder why we didn't warm up with the real thing: I mean, they were the same balls but with different graphics. Same weight, same size, everything. But, as I explained, the best footballers are very particular, and from that day on we warmed up with the real thing. And the minute Jürgen started his dive celebration he became an instant phenomenon – and his number 18 shirt became very sought-after property. The club shop sold so many Klinsmann replica shirts that they ran out of the letter 'N'. That was how popular he was. And it's why the number 18 shirt is still one of the most desirable shirts at Tottenham. I suppose to many it will always be 'Jürgen's number'.

I admit I wasn't chuffed when they brought in squad numbers. I thought it was much easier before 1994: you'd get the team sheet and the right back would wear 2, the centre halves wore 4 or 5, etc. But I soon realised the new rule cleared up a lot of mess with players wanting shirts in a specific size. Every player had his own shirt, in his size, and only one player wore one shirt.

But when certain players didn't get the right number, they would try to be creative and they would ask for numbers like 82 if they couldn't get 10 (8+2 = 10). But I had to put my foot down with a lot of those ideas, because I'm a purist. I remember we played a pre-season tour in South Africa and we played against an Orlando Pirates left-winger with the number 115. Now, I've never asked for a footballer's shirt in my career, until I met that bloke. I kept it as a souvenir, because triple figure was taking the mickey!

Numbers aside, some players are just as particular with sizes, even the smaller players sometimes ask for big kits, if they like a lot of movement. But Jermain Defoe was obsessed with small shirts at one time, and I was forever ordering him shirts two sizes smaller than the rest of the lads. Robbie Keane used to wear a 'medium', too, and he used to change his shirt more than most. We were with Kappa at that time and they ran out of their small sizes quite quickly. Robbie said to me, 'I've run out of small shirts,' and I said, 'Stop giving them away, then!'

SHIRTS, SHORTS & SPURS

Those Kappa shirts were the first skin-tight shirts, and the first season was really difficult for the lads. The average player would wear large or XL, but the equivalent of large in Kappa was XXXL. We were all over the place that season, and I often wonder how the fans survived... we had trouble squeezing finely tuned athletes into those shirts; I suppose if you liked a pie and a beer it was even harder.

It's a little-known fact that we have two secret touchline shirts at Spurs, and they're numbers 49 and 50. They're called 'blood shirts', because these two are the emergency kits that are thrown on should a player have an injury that makes them bleed on their shirt. As the Spurs kit is white, the slightest speck of blood shows on it, so the blood shirts are a necessary part of the kit. Away shirts were OK, but a bit of blood on the lily-white and you had to swap it quickly. I used to take four shirts to a game for each player: two long, two short. Four covers all eventualities, you see. But when there's blood involved, anything goes. Just ask Anthony Gardner, who in one game in 2003 got a bad cut and was bleeding from his head. Naturally, I threw on the blood shirt, number 49, but he was quickly bleeding again, and soon was wearing the 50. At half-time he was still bleeding terribly, so I gave him his spare but the claret was still pouring out from under the hastily applied bandages. I was running out of shirts quicker than Tony was running out of blood, and before long I was in the dressing room, ringing blood out of his shirts, in case he'd have to change again.

Luckily, he didn't, but he'd worn five shirts in one game – a record that still stands today.

In the old days, players would have one shirt to last them all season, and, once the shirts were finished with, the evening schoolboys would train in last year's kits, and then they'd get passed down again. I'd even known Johnny Wallis to cut up the old shirts and clean the boots with them, which is sacrilege really. Looking back, those beautiful, classic shirts being used as cleaning cloths should really have been in museums.

I'd been on the ground staff for a few months when Johnny was laying the kit out, and, being the true Spurs fan, he said, 'Come and have a look.'

I remember touching the shirts for the first time: the numbers were embroidered on. There were plain blue shorts, with plain white socks. Of course, as things progressed, the shirts got whiter and lighter, and the sponsors came in. I often liked to think what Johnny would have made of today's fancy designs, as I remember him cutting the feet off the socks to use them as a buffer to shine the boots. Johnny used to say that the players from his day were very superstitious and, thinking about it, so was he. You have to have a degree of OCD to be a kit man: it comes with the job, you want everything to be 'just so'.

Here I am talking about the players' superstitions, and I'm exactly the same! I always worked from behind the dressing-room door, left to right, round the dressing room, laying out the kit. That's the way I work. But the thing is, when you play at Wembley, the numbers go the wrong way! Instead of going left to right, it goes right to left, one, two, three... so I had to pack the kit back to front. When they put those numbers on the pegs at Wembley, it really ruined my routine. Because when things go wrong with the kit, everybody notices.

I had a couple of shirts come in wrong over the years. The manufacturer prints them up, and I've spotted a few misspellings, and pulled them out. But it's every kit man's nightmare. I remember watching Peter Crouch for England when he had 21 on his back and 12 on the front! I used to have a checklist to mark off to make sure everything was correct, and, if someone came in and asked for a sock or something, I put a ruler underneath my point on the list, or I'd have to shut the door and work through my second and third check alone.

When players place their superstitions in your hands, it really puts you under pressure. Teddy Sheringham would say before we left London for an away game, 'Don't forget to take my favourite shirt,' or 'Don't forget my Adidas moulds,' and I'd have a panic attack. I'd put everything on the coach, and double check, triple check, but I'd pull out of Spurs Lodge in the van and think, 'Did I pack those bloody moulded boots?' Of course, I'd get to the hotel, and pull the skip out... and I'd know it was there, but I'd get it out and the relief was amazing.

You see, as a kit man, you can't argue with a player's routine. Keeping the team happy was my number-one objective, no matter how silly or important the request. For example, the right studs can be game-changing. But the players don't realise just how long it takes to change 12 studs. I remember when we were playing Chelsea away in 1994, and Teddy trotted in from the warm-up, tossed me his boots and said, 'Roy, these boots aren't right, I need new studs.'

This wasn't 1.30pm; it was 2.50pm, with just minutes left before kick-off. And I got a 'turner'. Anyone that's ever had studded boots will know what a turner is: when the thread's gone, and the only way to sort them out is to hacksaw off the stud, knock the insert out and put a new stud in. 'OK, Ted,' I told him. 'Wait there.'

'The pressure's on,' he laughed.

I used to carry a portable vice for just this occasion, but, as I got busy with the vice and the hacksaw, I remembered that the more you panic, the longer it takes. While this is going on there's 14 other players asking for new shirts, or long sleeves, or a new sock, and I'm trying to hacksaw off a stud. At home I used to have an assistant but away I was on my own. I managed to give him his boots back with new studs with a minute left to kick-off, and Teddy scored the equaliser to salvage a point.

After Ted left Spurs for Manchester United, the White Hart Lane faithful changed his terrace song to 'Whoa Teddy, Teddy! He went to Man United and he won fuck all!' but he certainly showed them. The fans would later stop singing this, when Teddy returned to Spurs in 2001, having won the Premiership, the FA Cup and the Champions League with United, but we welcomed him back with open arms.

I'd had a great relationship with Teddy over the years, and I'll never forget the day he said to me quietly, 'Roysie, I need a special shirt made up.' Ted told me that he was teetering on the edge of scoring his 300th league goal, having reached 299 in all domestic competitions since starting his career with Millwall back in the 1980s. Should he score again, the 36-year-old would join his England teammate Alan Shearer in the exclusive '300 club', a remarkable achievement. 'Can you make me a special T-shirt to wear underneath my shirt?' he asked. 'I want something to remember the game by.'

As always, we were unprepared. I didn't have time to get the manufacturer to make up a special T-shirt with all the professional printing, so, as the team prepared to take on struggling Sunderland, I took a white Kappa vest, and with my trusty black marker pen I got to work in my little kit room.

'What have you got there, Roysie?' a couple of the players asked when I came out.

'Wait and see,' I told them, as I handed the shirt to Teddy, who slipped it on under his now famous number 10 jersey.

The thing is, he'd have to wait a few games to finally do it, and ended up wearing that special vest for quite some time. But at White Hart Lane on Saturday, 8

February 2003, in the 84th minute, Sheringham rose unguarded to head home a free header from a Darren Anderton corner, scoring Spurs' final goal in a 4–1 victory over Sunderland, and he became only the second striker after Shearer to achieve the feat of 300 English club football goals.

Sheringham celebrated by peeling off his top to reveal that vest, bearing the words '300 NOT OUT!!' He got a standing ovation, and I chuckled to myself as every newspaper showed the picture on the back pages the next morning. With a bit more time I could have made the handwriting a bit neater. You see, I will forever be a perfectionist.

Glenn Hoddle, who had brought Sheringham back to Spurs from Manchester United two years previously, summed it up when he said, 'Three hundred goals is a fantastic milestone, but people should sit back and think, "How many goals has he made for other players in his career as well?"' I couldn't agree more.

In studs or moulded boots, Ted was the calmest player I've ever worked with. He played that way too – he never looked rattled. But in fact, when he first came to Spurs, he became very superstitious when he went through a rare goal drought. At the time, he had never worn a long-sleeved shirt, for Forest or Millwall, and I always appreciated that his requirements were so predictable. But during this goal drought he confessed he didn't know what to do. So I said, 'Why don't you wear a long-sleeved shirt?' And he laughed, 'No way, Roysie.' But I gave him one, and he said he'd give it a try. And strangely enough he scored. You see, sometimes, psychologically, when you make a change, it can change your luck.

I remember seeing the front pages of all the newspapers the day after he won the Champions League Final (and the Treble) with Manchester United. In all the photographs, he had both arms raised in the air... in long sleeves, and I had a little chuckle to myself.

CHAPTER 11
EARNING THEIR SPURS

Over the years, I worked very closely with the young apprentices at Spurs, and later, when it became the Tottenham Hotspur Academy, I looked after the kits of all the young players whom the club were carefully nurturing. I used to watch all the games, and as such I came to recognise very early the ones who stood out, and perhaps young players who I suspected would never become Spurs legends. But there was one young boy who turned up at Tottenham's Academy – a floppy-haired youngster from Leytonstone –that all the coaches were particularly keen on. David, his name was.

This young man spent four years on the books at Tottenham Hotspur between 1987 and 1991, and when he left everyone was incredibly disappointed. When he was 14, David signed for Manchester United, a club he had confessed to me once were his favourite team. A few years later, I was watching *Match of the Day* and I saw that former Spurs kid score a goal for United from the halfway line, past Wimbledon's keeper, Neil Sullivan. His name, of course, was David Beckham. And I seem to recall he did rather well for himself after leaving Spurs.

But thousands of others didn't do so well. When I watched Beckham play as a kid at Spurs, he had that uncanny ability to get crosses in from ridiculous angles, to spray those Hollywood passes around the pitch – and all that as a youngster. Yet it was so hard to predict the ones that would make it and the ones who would be left on the scrapheap. It wasn't easy to make it back in my day, but it is even harder now: today the Tottenham Hotspur Academy coaches young footballers from the ages of 8 to 18, involving approximately 150 young players, looked after by 30 full-time and part-time staff. But if you look at the few who have made it – Ledley King, Glenn Hoddle, Peter Crouch, Stephen Carr, Nick Barmby, Ian Walker, Sol Campbell, David Howells and Tony Parks – you know how slim that success rate is.

In my day, you'd have just 30 Academy or 'apprentice' players, and a handful of them would get to play for the reserves on a Monday. You'd only get 15 games a season and, if they didn't shine, they'd be let go. Some of the kids I'd think, 'They're amazing,' or others you'd think, 'They're just not a Tottenham player.'

I always used to notice it was the players who had a certain arrogance that always made it. If they had a little bit of that right brand of cockiness, it showed on the pitch, particularly the goalkeepers. Without that bravery and confidence, a young keeper would get knocked about. It's why we were sometimes tough on the young players, and tested their attitudes, because, if you're released and packed off to Southend, you need to know what's going on in the real world. This was a familiar tale, because, if you had 15 Academy A-team players, maybe one or two would sign for one year or maybe three years, and only one of those players would make it to the first team. Seven or eight would get signed elsewhere, but, with a club as big as Spurs, there's only one way to go, and that's down. Very seldom does a player leave to go to another, bigger club.

I spent a lot of time with the apprentices when I first started at Spurs, and I was very close to the likes of Mark Bowen, Ian Crook, Paul Moran, Micky Hazard, Ian Culverhouse and Richard Cook. I watched them all grow up as apprentices, learning the sport, working hard, cleaning boots and becoming young men along the way. We used to have some big laughs and, although I was a bit older than them, we were like brothers. We'd create some mini games in the gym, and when I moved up to working for the reserves, so did they, and it was great for me to watch them progress and blossom. But for that particular generation of Spurs Youth, breaking into the first team would become 'mission impossible', for the team of the day contained some of the most unshakeable footballers, like Glenn Hoddle and Steve Perryman. I felt sorry for those young pretenders to the throne, because they just couldn't make it into the squad. If Glenn hadn't been there, players like Micky Hazard and Ian Crook would be household names today. But they still moved onwards and upwards, and I was delighted to watch all of those players make real names for themselves at other clubs.

Micky Hazard's ability on the ball and his dribbling was second to none. When he used to come and play five-a-side in the gym he embarrassed anyone who cared to try to tackle him. A frustrated Micky left Spurs, signed for Chelsea, then played at Portsmouth (under Ossie Ardiles) before returning to Tottenham in November 1993 for £50,000, where he would stay until his retirement in 1995. You probably don't remember, but it was Micky who began the 'liquid football' move that set up Jürgen Klinsmann's famous debut goal.

Ian Crook could hit a dustbin lid from 100 metres, but left Spurs in 1986 for Norwich City for just £80,000. There, he would become one of the club's biggest bargains and the lynchpin of the most successful team in Norwich's history. Mark Bowen left Spurs and later became an assistant manager at Blackburn, Manchester City and finally the Welsh squad under Mark Hughes, and is still enjoying a fine career as a coach. And Ian Culverhouse, after he picked up a winner's medal in the UEFA Cup (as an unused substitute for Spurs in the 1984 final against Anderlecht), became an assistant manager at Norwich City. I knew they'd all do well, but I would have preferred to see them all become legends at Spurs, a club they loved as much as I did. One of my most treasured items is a Christmas card from all of the aforementioned boys when they were apprentices, and I love hearing that they have done so well.

Stevie Perryman was the player they all wanted to be: a London boy who worked his way from the apprentices all the way to the first team, and a whole lot more. Steve's about five years older than me, but he always felt a *lot* older because he had this very mature head on his shoulders. I was only at Spurs a few months when he was in the Academy, and Steve broke into the first team at just 17, which was unheard of at the time. They gave him the number 8 shirt, and it didn't hit him till someone told him that he was wearing Jimmy Greaves' shirt. He soon moved to number 10 and then finally settled with number 6, which was another big shirt to fill: Dave McKay's. After 655 appearances, it's safe to say he made that shirt his own.

You could talk about the number of players to have come through the Spurs Academy who became Spurs captains and England Internationals in just one chapter, so exclusive is that club. Sol Campbell and Ledley King are the most obvious ones. I knew them both as boys, and watched them become grown men, Spurs legends, and finally I watched them net goals for their country. I remember Ledley as a very young kid, and he was from that era when those schoolboys were my responsibility. He played from 9 up to 15 as a schoolboy, then when he left school he started at Spurs full-time. When he turned 16, I kept an eye on him, and watching him play I suspected he had something the other kids didn't. When Ledley ran, he didn't look quick – somehow he looked like he was standing still – but he covered the ground so well. When Ledley was 14, he was as tall as he is today, so he stood out head-and-shoulders above the other players. And the way he played, he was never rattled and looked like a natural. All the coaches were very excited.

Ledley commanded the defence and he had fantastic discipline – excellent traits of known winners. But we didn't think in a million years he'd be a Spurs captain. You could never predict that. He did, however, coast reserve games, and, when he stepped up to the first team, that was the acid test. Ledley was still growing, and quickly stepped into the shadow of Sol Campbell, our then unshakeable defender.

Ledley's debut came in May 1999 at Anfield, no less, and, although the game ended in a 3–2 defeat to Liverpool, Ledders played well and George Graham was proud of him. But the former Arsenal manager used the London-born player as a midfielder at first, and, by the time Liverpool returned to play Tottenham at White Hart Lane, King had established himself as a first-team regular, and we beat them 2–1 in the November clash of 2000. The next month, his first goal for Tottenham came in a 3–3 draw away to Bradford City and was scored in just 10.2 seconds, setting a new Premier League record for the quickest goal. That goal etched Ledley King into the record books and, almost indelibly, into the first-team sheet for many games to come.

When Sol made the shocking move to rivals Arsenal, it was a gift for Ledley, and soon the White Hart Lane faithful started to sing, 'You can stick your Sol Campbell up your arse... 'cos we've got Ledley at the back!' I think they were right in a way, as everyone felt Ledley could, and would, become the next Sol Campbell. Ledders said to me once in my kit room, 'This is my chance, Roy, and I'm going to take it.' I had so much hope for Ledley, and I was beginning to think he might just become the next Stevie Perryman.

After George Graham was sacked, King was moved back into defence under new manager Glenn Hoddle, and set about making himself one of the best centre-backs Spurs had ever seen. Ledders began that season with a clean sheet against Aston Villa and a superb performance man-marking Duncan Ferguson that allowed Spurs to hold on for a point against Everton at Goodison Park. Then, just two years after making his Spurs debut, Ledley was capped for England and was regarded as one of the best young defenders in the country, as Tottenham finished ninth – our highest league finish in six years. To this day, I think he's one of the finest defenders in Spurs' history. I watched them all at White Hart Lane – Morris Norman, when I was a little kid, then Graham Roberts – but in my opinion Ledley is the pick of the bunch.

I still get such a big kick out of watching Ledley play, and when I see him making those massive strides across the back four, swooping in to save Spurs with one of those brave challenges, I can't help but think back to those magnificent performances he put in as a kid, playing at the Academy. I'm still close to Ledley, and he often sends me tickets to home games, so I can come and watch him play.

Working with the apprentices and the Academy used to give me cause for complaint, as, when you're folding up your thousandth kid-sized Tottenham shirt, sometimes you'd wonder why you bother: the success rate is so slight. But it helps to watch Ledley King play, and remember where he came from. I suppose, in a way, Sol's surprising move to that club down the road was a blessing in disguise for Ledley King. Because, had he spent much more time in Sol's shadow, perhaps he'd have ended up like a Bowen, a Crook, a Hazard or a Culverhouse – forced to go and blossom elsewhere.

To go over the road to Arsenal was a massive decision for Sol, and very few have ever done the reverse: Pat Jennings, Neil Jenkins and Jimmy Robertson are the only ones that spring to mind. But you must remember that Pat came the other way because Arsenal said they didn't want him any more. Now that's a different story. It was different with Sol, and most unusual for a Spurs player to willingly leave for our hated rivals, Arsenal. I was chuffed when Sol started captaining the side, because in the reserves, just like Ledley, Sol was so laidback. I remember thinking, 'This lad could be a bit special.'

Say what you like about Sol, until he made that decision

to go, he was outstanding for Spurs. I loved Sol Campbell, and no one anticipated he was going to leave the club like he did. Right up until the night before the decision was announced, he was telling me, 'I'm staying, Roysie.' From there, he was sold to Portsmouth for a considerably higher fee of £1.25 million, and the lanky striker scored 18 league goals in 37 starts for Portsmouth, before moving to Liverpool via stints at Southampton and Aston Villa, and then finally signing for Spurs, again, in 2009.

When I found out he had signed for our arch rivals, I was shocked. I thought he was Spurs through and through, and I'd taken it for granted that Sol Campbell would be at Spurs forever.

But sometimes players did leave and like Sol went on to make a success of themselves elsewhere. Peter Crouch is a good example – an Academy player who was released, and who went on to sign professional terms at another club. I remember Crouchy because he stood out being a foot taller than every other kid on the books! All the kit he tried on as a schoolboy was too small, so I used to give him one of the first-team shirts, because even as a lad he was as tall as an adult player. Even today, if you look at him playing for Spurs you'll see that the kit never fits him properly. His England shirts are different, they're hand-made for him by Umbro's Savile Row tailors, but the Spurs shirts always come up short.

Peter got as far as the Spurs reserve team and then, on 28 July 2000, Tottenham sold him to Queens Park

Rangers for just £60,000. He made an immediate impression with the West Londoners, scoring ten league goals in the 2000/01 season, but it was not enough to prevent the team's relegation to what is now Football League One. From there, he was sold to Portsmouth for a considerably higher fee of £1.25 million, and the lanky striker scored 18 league goals in 37 starts for Portsmouth, before moving to Liverpool and then finally signing for Spurs, again, in 2009. It goes to show, sometimes, even though you might have to go a roundabout route, it's not over for a player once they've been released by the Academy.

In my day, there was a big impetus on the youth system, because back then it was more important to bring young players through the ranks, even if it was just to sell them on and make a profit. We had a scouting system headed up by former Spurs legend John Moncur, and the club would have scouts all over the country watching schoolboy games. A lad would get recommended and, because they couldn't invite every boy along to train, Spurs would deploy a scout to go and watch the kid play. The club would request his next three fixtures and the venues, and someone would come down. We had the best scouts in England, and our senior scouts would go and watch professional games with an eye on any young player that could be poached.

But today the game is such a multi-million-pound business, you can't really afford to feed someone into the first team from the Academy. You can't afford to give them ten games to settle in, and let them make their mistakes on the biggest stage in English football. Teams like Tottenham Hotspur need immediate success, and places on the team can be quickly and efficiently filled by making shrewd purchases – not by watching a young kid develop for a decade. Look at the team today and our young stars – Huddlestone was bought from Derby, and Danny Rose was purchased from the Leeds Academy after they'd done much of the hard work – and look at how it paid off.

Danny Rose made his league debut against Arsenal on 14 April 2010, and his first goal was described in *The Times* as 'a volley so thunderous that you could hear the whack off his boot above the din of the raucous crowd'. The wondergoal was hailed the strike of the season by commentator Andy Gray, but, most importantly, it won Spurs the game 2–1 and helped secure that vital Champions League spot. Danny Rose cost us 'in the region of £1m', which, in the long run, is a comparative bargain. And what a goal! If you were going to score just one goal, and past one team, and never play again, you'd want it to be that goal.

Today the Spurs Academy features a network of 35 scouts who are tasked with finding the best local, national and international talent. It's proving to be worth its weight in gold, as we're bringing forward young players like Jake Livermore and Andros Townsend. But you'd be shocked at how stringent and tough the selection process is for even a nine-year-old potential Spurs player. According to the 'Tottenham Hotspur Player Pathway', junior recruits to the club are spotted through 'Talent' football courses, before being invited to train at a development centre, where their talents are fully judged. From there, they progress to an 'Elite Centre' which trains on a Friday afternoon at Spurs Lodge, and again on Saturday morning at Myddleton House, before they are put through a tough 'Friday Assessment' every six weeks at the official Spurs training complex. Then, after a gruelling six-week 'Academy Trial', they can be accepted into the U9+ Academy. All this before they even reach the age of ten! As I said before, this is big business, and hopefully we won't let a young man like David Beckham slip through our fingers again.

CHAPTER 12

LEGENDS AT THE LANE

Ask me about my most memorable games at White Hart Lane, and I'll tell you about one surprising match that I bet you probably didn't even see. It was played on a bitterly cold October evening in 2002, and was billed as a 'Tottenham Tribute Match' against American side DC United. The game was designed to raise money for ex-Spurs players suffering from hardship, of which there are far too many, in my experience. And with them playing in all white, the Spurs team that night was as close to any fan's 'dream team' as could be possible, with countless living legends turning up for the game. Well, I've never laid out a dressing room like it. I have a photograph of it that I call the 'legends corner', which really is quite special.

Before the game, I hung up the shirts of one Spurs hero after another, one-by-one, sighing to myself with disbelief

153

as the shirts came out of the kit bag: Sheringham, Klinsmann, Hoddle, Allen, Ginola, Allen, Waddle and, my all-time hero, Paul Gascoigne. Then the dressing room soon filled with luminaries from generations of Spurs teams. As a stickler for detail, I was somewhat disturbed that there were two number 10 shirts, but, when Sheringham and Hoddle were to play on the same team, I had to let it slide!

Teddy was one of the best footballers I've ever seen. His football brain was notoriously developed, and he had the perfect nature for a footballer. I don't think I ever saw Teddy rant and rave in the dressing room, until he became captain, and then he used to say a fair bit. But Teddy had a way of articulating himself that always made complete sense. Let's be honest, Ted didn't have a lot of pace but he was always in the right place at the right time, with that half-a-yard advantage and that natural ability that made him a world champion.

Players didn't often come back to Spurs once they had left. And I was desperately unhappy when Teddy left at the end of the 2002/03 season. I didn't want him to go because he was our best player. In his last ever game against Blackburn Rovers, it was very emotional. I remember we wore the next year's kit as a preview – a baby-blue Kappa away strip. It was the commercial department being clever, and they were doing 'pre-sales' in the club shop after the game. In our new kit, it was a clear sign that we were thinking ahead to the future, but it would be a future that wouldn't include

Teddy Sheringham, whose contract was terminated after the game.

He was a closed book for most of the time, but it was clear that Teddy was emotionally moved during his last game. It must have been difficult for him to leave the club he had such an affinity for, particularly as it was the club who decided not to renew his contract. Spurs said at the time that their move to ditch the 37-year-old former England International was made with an 'eye on the future', but everyone, from the staff to the supporters, was disappointed. Portsmouth quickly snapped him up, and I remember the cold Monday night in October 2004 when Spurs played Teddy's new team, Pompey, at Fratton Park: they beat us 1–0 and Teddy played a blinder. Afterwards, he stuck his head around the away dressing-room door and threw his Pompey shirt at me. When I got it home, he'd written on the white number 10: 'Dear Roysie, I hope you're still smiling!'

I suppose, in a way, Teddy had just as strong a claim to the number 10 shirt as Glenn Hoddle that evening against DC United. Glenn had just broken into the first team when I joined Spurs, and I can tell you that there are not many people with his ability in both feet. For the majority of people, their standing leg is wooden, and kicking with it is like a golf swing – nothing bends! But Glenn could take a penalty, a corner or hit a 60-yard cross-field pass with either foot and it would be amazing. Even when I was a player I couldn't use my right foot, I'd always try to shift it on to my left, and I'd wish I could kick it like Glenn.

Glenn could hit Tony Galvin with the football from 70 yards, every time, and one ball I remember seeing him hit at White Hart Lane was something else entirely. It was pouring with rain, and somehow Glenn hit it with some kind of magical backspin. This ball caught the surface, and instead of doing what the laws of gravity demanded – which was zip out into the West Stand – it stuck to the touchline like a magnet. If you'd hit a golf shot like that, you'd pack up your clubs and never play again. They used to say on the terraces at White Hart Lane, 'Glenn Hoddle can walk on water.' And I could believe it.

The best goal I ever saw him score was at Watford. He chipped a 6'7" goalkeeper with such ease, yet there was only one place for the ball, which was wedged in the stanchion, and that was where he left it. Before this game against DC United, playing for the Spurs Legends, his last goal for Spurs was also something magical. Glenn ran from the halfway line, beat two defenders, dropped his shoulder – and his body swerve was so convincing the keeper dived out the way, and he slotted the ball home. If there's a way to go, that was it. I wonder if he remembered it as he came in the dressing room that October evening, and saw his number 10 shirt hanging up at White Hart Lane for the first time in 15 years. 'Hello, Roysie,' he smiled, and shook my hand warmly. I was having a nice evening.

I suppose Glenn came back to play the DC United

game for a laugh, and I think it was just too much to resist, playing in front of a packed crowd at White Hart Lane, but unfortunately a calf strain prevented him from playing. As the game kicked off, the skills on show that night were so much cleverer than you'd see at a competitive match. And the game quickly took on a real party atmosphere. White Hart Lane was alive like I'd never seen it before, and I watched as four Mexican waves rippled around the stadium. Even the people in the directors' box joined in. Gazza was doing kick-ups on the halfway line; he laid the ball off to Klinsmann, who suddenly put Clive Allen through on goal. You had to see it to believe it.

Clive was a goal machine in his day, and for David Pleat's side he once scored 49 goals in one season... playing up front on his own. We played five in midfield in those days and 'Chesney' Allen, as we used to call him, was up front. Everything he touched flew in the net, and, as a finisher, he was second to none. I'd worked at Ossie Ardiles' testimonial a few years previously, and Clive played up front alongside Diego Maradona and that was another one of those nights where anything could happen.

I can see Diego now, in my dressing room. I was standing by my kit-room door, and Diego got changed where the number 9 shirt would be, which was actually Clive Allen's shirt, but I suppose he didn't complain that night! You should have seen Maradona in his shorts – his legs were carved out of granite, zero fat, just muscle, like nothing I'd ever seen. We used to have fruit on the table in those days, and Maradona started juggling an orange with his bare feet. He was talking to people and signing autographs, all the time juggling this orange – and it didn't touch the floor once. I was mesmerised.

Of course, Diego had turned up with no boots and, typically, there was a panic on with just moments before kick-off. I asked Diego and he said, 'I'm a size 6, but I must wear Puma because they pay me a lot of money.'

Surprisingly, there weren't an abundance of size-6 Puma boots in the kit room, and I was about to get my paintbrush out again, when suddenly Clive Allen said, 'I've got a spare pair of size-6 Puma Kings here.'

So, disaster was averted again, and Diego played in a Spurs shirt, a photo of which has become a teasing reminder to Spurs fans of what could have been. The match was fantastic, and Diego came in after the game and gave Clive his boots back. Puma Kings at the time had the big white floppy tongues that were de rigueur of the day, and Diego signed the boots, 'To Clive, thanks for the boots, from Diego Maradona.'

Clive was chuffed to bits. Years later I spoke to him while he was in the middle of moving house. He confessed that he'd looked for the boots while he was packing, and asked his wife if she'd seen them. 'Those old boots with the writing on?' she'd said. 'I threw them out!' Clive, panicking, hunted through all the rubbish bins, and luckily he found those boots. But it was a close call.

Clive played alongside Ginola in that DC United game,

two of the fastest and most skilful footballers we've ever had. I used to really admire Ginola, and he was one of my favourite Spurs players of that era. One afternoon we had a game of crossbar challenge. The lads were training and David stepped out for a bit. I had grabbed ten balls and put them along the 18-yard line, and I was kicking balls at the bar, and doing all right. Ginola walked across and said, 'I'll play.'

We took five balls each, and I was up for the challenge. I hit my first ball quite sweetly and clipped the top of the bar. To say I was pleased with myself was an understatement. David missed his first kick, and I was feeling confident. He was kicking with his supposed weak foot, but with the next four balls he hit the bar so sweetly, so damned precisely, that the ball would return right back at his foot with a huge clang. It was an amazing demonstration of pure talent. I didn't kick any more balls that day.

Sat in the dugout, where I watched decades of football, is the only place you can really appreciate David Ginola, because he spent his entire time at White Hart Lane running up and down that touchline, mostly with the ball stuck to his foot like it was on Velcro. You had to wonder how on earth he carried on with some of the challenges. Lesser players would try to wipe him out, and he'd mug them right off.

I'd sit there and think, 'The next one's going to take you round the neck.' When he came in at half-time, his legs were cut to ribbons, and we used to have to patch him up, but he would always carry on. 'New socks please, Roysie,' he'd say, in his fantastic Gallic accent.

Ginola scored a goal in the quarter-final of the FA Cup – against Barnsley away, on Tuesday, 16 March 1999 – that would redefine everyone's definition of a world-class goal. A writer in the *Independent* would claim his goal was enough 'to rival Ricky Villa's endlessly replayed slalom through Manchester City's defence in the final replay of 18 years ago'. And he was right: it was one of the most unbelievable goals in living memory, with the Frenchman cutting in from the left wing, slipping through four attempted tackles. Then, 12 yards before goal, he slotted the ball past a hapless Tony Bullock and into the far corner of the net, sending the travelling Spurs fans absolutely delirious.

The problem was, David ran to the fans and threw his shirt in the crowd, which ordinarily wouldn't have been a problem, as this was before the FA's needless automatic booking rule. But this was the second half and David was already on his second shirt, and his first was lying soaking wet on the dressing-room floor. Thankfully, the Spurs fan that caught it was persuaded by the Frenchman to throw it back, but Ginola was still trying to get it on when the game restarted. Luckily, he could continue to embarrass the ill-equipped Barnsley with his outrageous skills. I breathed a sigh of relief.

I can't talk about Spurs legends without mentioning Gary Mabbutt. Gary was diabetic, and, although I don't understand a lot about the condition, I knew Mabbsy wasn't going to let it control his football career. In the dressing room before the game, he'd sit there taking his blood levels. I'd watch him prick his finger and use a little machine to read his blood-sugar level. The read-out on the screen would determine how much Lucozade he needed, and then he'd be ready for action, and, apart from one blip, it never affected his career. There was one game where he just didn't turn up and the club phoned ex-player John Lacey who was a good friend of Gary's. John found him in his house, alone, collapsed on the floor. We were very worried, but fortunately it all turned out well in the end.

But apart from this, his condition never changed the way he played football. Gary became an England player, and of course he captained Spurs and lifted the FA Cup. I remember I used to get Gary's boots repaired, because he had less feeling in one of his feet due to the diabetes, and he wouldn't know if he had a blister. So he kept the same pair of Adidas for years! There was a cobbler not far from the ground, and he mended Gary's boots every other weekend. I think Mabbsy kept him in business to be honest, as after Gary left the shop closed down!

Back to the DC United game, and Klinsmann was full of energy and enthusiasm, running at the American defence with aplomb. Gazza was just a shadow of his former self, and was lacking that exciting skill for which the Spurs fans had come to love him. But he was cheered wildly with every touch, and played up to the crowd like it was

1991 again. The crowd were invited to vote for their man of their match by texting in on their mobile phones, and the result was David Ginola, who brought back many happy memories by embarking on a few of those meandering runs.

Naturally, Gazza, Klinsmann and Ginola received great ovations when they left the field at White Hart Lane, but there was to be no charity from the visitors who persisted in attacking Lars Hirshfeld's goal – Hirshfeld had to make even more saves than Keller had in the first half. Olsen hit the bar with a chipped shot and the follow-up was put in the net, but the friendly linesman had his flag up. Rebrov replaced Sheringham, but DC United had clearly not read the script for such occasions, as their striker Barrett scored a late winner, beating us 1–0 in front of a home crowd.

That night it seemed like there were too many Spurs legends to fit into one team, and needless to say I suppose a few who wanted to play were left out. However, I shall not leave out some contenders for my own personal dream team here. Chris Hughton would always be on my team sheet. He was a lift engineer before he joined Spurs, and he wouldn't sign until he'd finished his apprenticeship! It was a good grounding for a career at Spurs, the lift-engineering game. He knew all about ups and downs! Chris was a very slight player, a right or left back, and a very honest athlete who started in Keith's era and never left. Like myself, Chris was Spurs through and through. He even stepped in as caretaker manager on a couple of occasions, and eventually he got his break with Martin Jol. What did Jol see in Chris? He saw Spurs. You only associate Chris with the club, and for that the supporters will always love him.

With 27,000 supporters packed into White Hart Lane for that DC United match, Spurs would have raised over £250,000 for former players who had fallen on hard times. I saw it first-hand at Spurs – how some players arrived just on the cusp of the big money, the Sky television cameras, the boot sponsorship and the million-pound transfer fees. I worked with players like Micky Hazard, who I think was one of the most talented players we ever had. As I've said before, he couldn't replace Glenn Hoddle, and who could? Today, while many of the players who have played alongside him are driving Bentleys and Ferraris, Micky Hazard drives a London taxi.

CHAPTER 13

TOUGH GUYS AND HARD MEN

I saw some horrendous injuries in my time. With players like Vinnie Jones arriving at White Hart Lane, you knew the physio was going to have a very busy day, and, from my view in the dugout, I saw 30 years of late challenges, dirty two-footed tackles and head-butts. And sometimes the away team were quite bad too!

The FA Cup Final against Manchester City in 1981 was mostly memorable for Villa's amazing goal, but Graham Roberts will remember it for another reason: he had his teeth kicked out by team-mate Chris Hughton as they both went for the same ball! They had to search through the grass to find those teeth, but of course Roberts played on like nothing had happened. They were all real men in those days.

I found myself on the back pages of the newspapers on 24 November 1993 when Gary Mabbutt was fouled so badly by John Fashanu that several of the staff had to help the St John Ambulance people carry him off on a stretcher. Fashanu caught him right in the face, and the blow literally caved in his cheekbone. Gary lifted his head up as we stretchered him to safety, and he said, 'I'm fine! I want to play on!' But as he looked at me, the right side of his face was completely concave. He had to have his face rebuilt with a mesh under the skin and had his eye socket remoulded. It's amazing the bloke is walking today, the amount of injuries I've seen him take.

Gary broke his leg at Blackburn, and I remember hearing it go. He was left-footed, and when the ball came down the line he went to hook it and clear the danger, but an attacker's studs clattered into his kicking leg, snapping his shin. He had no feeling, and as he stood up it audibly snapped. I felt sick to my stomach. Yet football is a contact sport, and for me the rough and tumble, the tackles and the blood and the tears are all part of the beautiful game.

Of course, I watched the game change over the 29 seasons I worked for Tottenham Hotspur. When I first started watching Spurs play, Dave Mackay and Alan Mullery were in the team – two players no one would want to mess with. Dave was such a big strong player, he'd just rattle through people and could run through brick walls. You've probably seen that famous photo in the club shop of him grabbing Billy Bremner by the scruff of the neck. Well, that picture sums up everything about Mackay, but what you must remember was that the Leeds team were the dirtiest team of that decade. Mackay had the bull by the horns.

Revie's men were a very physical side, earning the nickname 'Dirty Leeds', and there was one particularly memorable match against Derby, during which Leeds' Norman Hunter and Derby's Francis Lee had a fight. It wasn't a scrap; it was a full-blown boxing match. It started on the halfway line and went up into the penalty box, and they were still arguing when they were being booked. They got up and all of a sudden the commentator shouted, 'They're at it again!' and the fight continued!

Leeds hard men such as Bremner and Norman 'Bites Yer Legs' Hunter sent shivers down the spines of opponents. As well as fighting Lee, Hunter was also involved in a number of notorious punch-ups during his career, including during a Cup Winners' Cup Final defeat to Milan, meaning he'd had thrown more punches in his football career than some fighters did in their boxing careers. This was the era in which I entered football, as a kid stood up behind a navy-blue barrier at White Hart Lane, watching the visiting hard men do battle with my heroes. Every team had a tough guy. Chelsea had Ron 'Chopper' Harris, Leeds had Bremner and Hunter. It was essential to have a tough nut in those days, because if the going gets tough you need someone to bail you out.

When I first joined Tottenham Hotspur, we had four of them: Steve Perryman, Graham Roberts, Paul Miller and Terry 'Nutty' Naylor. Steve had a fantastic reputation as a footballer and a gentleman, but at one game in particular, away to Real Madrid, I learned that it wasn't wise to mess with the young man from Ealing. Spurs were attempting to defend our UEFA title in 1985 when Real Madrid beat us 1–0 at White Hart Lane, and it was the Spurs captain Steve Perryman who scored an own goal. One of the Spanish players, a left-winger, took a liberty with Stevie: something was said or there was a tackle that was over the top. Either way, it clearly stuck in the defender's mind.

On the return fixture in Spain, it was 0–0 with five minutes to go, when Perryman struck. A 50–50 ball flew up at about waist height between Stevie and that same Spanish winger. Well, Perryman took about five steps and flew into the player, absolutely destroying him. And with that, he walked straight off, not even waiting to see the inevitable flash of red card from the referee. We were out of the UEFA Cup, but Perryman had refused to lose a personal battle.

Paul Miller was another tough tackling defender who, like Stevie, had come through the ranks. Paul was like the original centre half, he'd head anything, kick anything, tackle anything; if he heard the grass rustle, he'd tackle it. During one game at the Lane, Miller had had an altercation with a player when the ball went up the other end, a looping, 70-yard ball that everyone followed with

y photo of the perfect combination: the FA Cup and a shirt from the 1991 final.

Above: Tense times on the bench during the 1991 FA Cup Final against Nottingham forest.

© *Getty Ima*

Below: Yet another celebration in the Wembley dressing room.

bove left: Another year, another photo of me with the FA Cup. Get the tash!

bove right: Defeat at the hands of Arsenal in the FA Cup Semi Final, 1993.
nd they say footballers don't care.

elow: Carrying Mabbsy off at White Hart Lane after his clash with John Fashanu.

The boot room at White Hart Lane – it hasn't changed that much over the years, even if I have! If you look at the more recent picture (*below*) you can see the door that Gazza riddled with his air rifle.

Watching from the sidelines…

Above: With Alan Harris celebrating a goal away from home.

Middle: 'Pass, pass, pass, pass!' That was always Ossie's way.

Below: Chrissie, me, Stevie P and Tony the physio, hard at work.

Above: Legends corner – the Spurs dressing room before the DC United friendly.

Below: Another legend.

Above: My first trip to South Africa with Tottenham Hotspur, with Jamie Redknapp (*back row, right*).

Below: Celebrating a goal with Martin Jol and Chrissie.

Above: Me with Ossie and Ricky, my two Argentinean friends!

Below: At my new home, Saracens' training ground.

their eyes. When their eyes came back to the pitch there was a centre forward sprawled out on the floor in our box –flattened when no one was looking.

Graham Roberts was the third of our four hard men from that era, and a player I greatly admired, because he made it to the top from the very bottom of the non-leagues, a feat that doesn't happen any more. 'Robbo', as friends knew him, had been released by Southampton but then worked his way up the leagues and signed for Spurs. He went on to captain Spurs against Anderlecht in the UEFA Cup Final, and his career was fresh from the pages of *Roy of the Rovers*. And for that reason he played every game like it was his last.

When Roberts first started at Spurs, he was a big, thickset lad, with huge tree-trunk legs and a swashbuckling style. But scrapping it out in the lower divisions had toughened him up, and David Pleat recognised that in him. Roberts was bossing the non-league. As soon as he arrived at White Hart Lane, he looked like a first-team player. It wasn't arrogance, but the minute he started playing he seemed like a winner – but he was also tough as old nails.

Once, I was in the tunnel at Highbury as the players lined up to run out for another heated North London derby. It was a very narrow tunnel in those days, and Spurs and Arsenal lined up shoulder-to-shoulder. Charlie Nicholas was playing for Arsenal, and Robbo, turning to team-mate Miller while staring at Nicholas, said, 'You chip him up and I'll volley him.' Charlie said, 'Good one, mate.' But Robbo gave him an icy stare and said, 'If you come anywhere near me, I'll smash you.'

Well, the game kicked off and within two seconds the ball flew up and trouble was brewing. Charlie tried to chest it, but instead Robbo sort of rabbit-punched him and Nicholas flew into the moat that surrounded the pitch! In those days you'd get one chance before getting the yellow card, and this was a typical welcome to the game from one of Tottenham's toughest ever players.

Another of our tough nuts was Terry Naylor, who played for the club until 1979. Previously, he was employed as a meat porter at London's Smithfield Market, and with his tough, uncompromising style of play he soon earned the nickname 'Meathook' with the White Hart Lane faithful. The staff used to call him 'Nutty Naylor' – for this very slight and slim cockney lad never shirked a challenge in his career. He was a crazy horse, and never jumped out of the way, the type of player you could do with in a Premiership side today. The difference being that today the game is so quick that most bad challenges aren't even intentional, unlike in Naylor's day when the odd rabbit punch was allowed.

Even our goalkeeper in those days was hard. Ray Clemence was tough as old boots, and, of all the goalkeepers I ever worked with, he was one of my favourites. Goalkeepers are never the full shilling! I don't know one keeper that's 'right' in the head. They've got this nuts way about them... and let's be honest, when the ball is ten feet in the air, and you've got to jump in with the feet flying and stick your head there, you've got to be insane. Look at Chelsea's Petr Cech: he nearly got killed at Reading when Hunt unintentionally left his foot in. It's a godforsaken position, because if you pull off a great save, you're half expected to do it, but if you let one through your legs, everyone jumps on your back.

Clemence was a magnificent goalkeeper, and, as Doug Livermore used to say, 'It's because he's mad!' Doug was right. 'Clem', as we called him, didn't have any fear factor at all. I've lost count of the number of times I watched Clem come out and take man and ball together, and I'm not always talking about the opposition. Clemence signed for Spurs as a 30-year-old, and was in no way a spring chicken, but he had this aura about him that was indescribable. He was 6'2", and when he walked out on to the field he just looked massive in the goal. With so much authority, he marshalled the Spurs defence like no other, as well as commanding respect. He used to fly out with his knee up, and put that knee in someone's chest while he caught the ball. He was caught really badly once by a player, and came hobbling back into the dressing room at half-time. I said, 'Are you all right, Clem?' and he said through gritted teeth, 'I'm fine, Roy, but let me tell you, every dog has his day.'

The goalkeeper didn't have to wait long for his revenge: in the second half that same player broke through, one-on-one with Clemence, when the whistle blew for offside. But foolishly the player carried on running, and Clemence simply destroyed him. He crashed through him so hard the player did three somersaults before hitting the ground. Where he remained for some time.

Goalkeepers in the old days were born hard. There was the famous occasion when Bert Trautmann played in a cup final with a broken neck. Our keeper Milija Aleksic, who played in the 1981 Cup Final, also showed that he was braver than most: we were playing away at Coventry and someone had a shot that flew over the bar, so he jumped up to make sure of it. But one of the hooks that hold the net up went into this leg, and as he fell it tore his leg all the way down. It was absolutely horrible. Who'd be a goalkeeper?

Later on, as the years progressed, we had fewer hard men per team, but those we had really put it about. In the 1990s, one of those players was Pat Van Den Hauwe. A footballing mongrel, Pat was born in Belgium, raised in Millwall and played for Wales, and was captured perfectly by author Ivan Ponting who wrote of Pat, 'He took to the pitch growling, scowling and stubbly, like some villainous refugee from a low-budget spaghetti western – and there is no shortage of opposing players and fans who reckoned he continued in similar vein once the game started.'

Sometimes, you had to watch Pat playing a match from behind your hands, and some of his performances should have carried a government health warning, but by God could he tackle. I certainly wouldn't have wanted to find myself with the ball in my possession with Pat Van Den Hauwe tearing towards me. He had the most terrifying eyes in English football and he could tackle you with a dirty look sometimes.

Earning the reputation of one of the hardest men in the division, Pat was dubbed 'Psycho-Pat' by Everton fans, his previous club before he joined Spurs. Soon after he arrived I would witness a battle between him and the only other player in the league to have earned the 'Psycho' moniker, when we played Nottingham Forest in 1989.

Stuart Pearce was an uncompromising left back, to put it mildly. I remember in the first half, the ball ran down the by-line, fast and loose, and suddenly Pat and Stuart were running headlong towards it, at speed. The whole stadium held their breath.

They hit each other full on, and the sound was like a big 'crash!'

The ball didn't even move as they hit each other like speeding juggernauts, and at half-time they limped back into the dressing room, putting a brave face on it.

'How you doing, Pat?' I asked, and he just said, 'Fine, I'm fine.'

And when we ran out after half-time, I said to the Forest physio, 'How's Pearce?' and he said, 'Fine, just fine.' And we looked at each other, and then he said, 'Actually, no, he's in pieces!' and I said, 'So is Pat!'

Luckily, I would never have to get involved in a player scrap like that on the pitch, but other kit men were not so lucky. I watched with horror on 25 January 1995 as Manchester United's kit man, Norman Davies, a friend of mine, fought to placate a certain angry Frenchman at Crystal Palace's ground, Selhurst Park. Norman was trying to pull Eric Cantona back as the player was sent off for a routinely aggressive challenge on Shaw. But Norm was raggy-dolled by Cantona, who steamed into the crowd and famously kung-fu-kicked a fan. I decided then I'd never get involved should that ever happen at Spurs!

But while Tottenham were aggressive and we had our own brand of hard men, we were never scandalous. I remember Mauricio Taricco could be a bit naughty, but because he wasn't very big he'd have to look after himself. Taricco would be running towards his own goal, on the edge of the box, with a striker putting pressure on him, and then somehow he'd trip over and lie on the ball! It became his trademark move, and he'd do it most weeks. If he got the free-kick, it was brilliant, and, if he didn't, he'd sit on the ball. It was a bit tricky, but it worked for him. It made the opposition very frustrated, and often they'd take it out on Taricco, making it a vicious cycle.

Of course, we never had our own Eric Cantona incident at White Hart Lane, although I can reveal something of the 'sportsmanship' that comes with hosting Premiership football matches, and 'welcoming' opposition players to the stadium. All the clubs were at it, like West Ham, who would turn the heating up to full in the dressing room and remove the radiator knobs when you played against them in the summer. Or another Northern club who would run the bath, but shut the doors. The place would be full of steam at half-time so you couldn't see each other, and all the clothes would be ringing wet.

We could be tricky at White Hart Lane, too. I remember when the Crazy Gang, Wimbledon FC, came to play during the famous times of John Fashanu and Vinnie Jones. They used to have this ghetto blaster and were the first team I remember who would take music with them to away games. That first afternoon they turned up, the music went on full with a 'Thud! Thud! Thud!' It was ear-splitting. So the ground staff said, 'Right, we'll turn the power off on the sockets,' and suddenly it went deathly quiet! Next thing we knew, their kit man ran round to the corner shop, bought ten packs of batteries and suddenly the music was back on, and twice as loud!

It would all go off in the tunnel before the game too. You'd hear it all: 'Your mum this' and 'Your wife that'. You'd be surprised what professional footballers say to each other before a game, particularly players that are International teammates, but especially when players had just faced each other in International tournaments.

I've often thought it nice that, for a club with such a large Jewish contingent, the fans' welcoming of

German players, ever since Jürgen Klinsmann really, has been nothing short of admirable. Our German signings have been among our toughest and strongest players, and certainly in the likes of Christian Ziege, our German left back, and Steffen Freund, our central midfielder, some of the hardest footballers of the decade. In one game for Spurs, after a tough clash, Ziege got a haematoma, like a swelling and internal bleeding on his thigh. He managed to play on in the second half but tragically he got hit again and had to come off. Back in the dressing room, we were icing it, and icing it, but it didn't look good, and we were so concerned we told him to call the doctor at any time during the night if it worsened. Well, Christian called the doc in the middle of the night, and when he arrived at Christian's house he had to operate immediately: the internal bleeding was so severe that had it been left any longer it could have been fatal. Now that was a strong challenge.

One of the most horrendous injuries I ever saw at White Hart Lane happened to visiting player Lee Chapman. Steve Sedgley and Chapman clashed when the West Ham player tried to trap the ball on his chest, and Sedgley came through and knocked him clean out. Chapman was unconscious before he even hit the floor, and slid face first into the red gravel running track that used to circle the pitch. He just skidded on his face, and it was one of the most awful things I've ever seen. When they finally got him up, Chapman's face was mangled, like something from a horror movie, and they were picking out the red shingle from his skin.

In the same era, Les Ferdinand was also a brave toe rag. 'Sir Les', to me, was the original gentleman and one of my favourite Spurs players of that generation. With his helicopter, suave attitude and manners, Sir Les was the black James Bond! As a person, he was an absolutely magnificent man, and, if you've ever watched tapes of him scoring goals for Spurs, QPR or even Newcastle, you'll notice that he had this uncanny ability to hang in the air. He'd jump earlier than everyone else, and stay up there, somehow.

But when he had his hair cut short, you could see that his head was covered with a myriad scars, a network of souvenirs of clashes with some of the Premiership's most horrible defenders. Once, he'd got his head cut open again, and in the dressing room at half-time the doctor was looking very concerned. He told me to hold a towel on to Les's head, and apply pressure, as the deep cut was gushing blood. Les sat on the couch, and as I took the towel off, he said, 'How bad is it, Roysie?'

I took one look under the towel, and I saw a gash an inch and a half long and an inch wide, and inside I could see his skull.

'It's not too bad!' I said cheerily, sickened to my stomach.

I watched the doctor stitch it, with no anaesthetic. It was pure adrenaline that got Les through it, and he got up, ran out and scored a header in the second half. Now, if I even have a blood test, I start to feel a bit queasy, whereas these guys are so brave. They just want to get back on to the field as quick as possible.

There are, of course, different types of tough guys. There are those who will stick their head in where no one else would dare, those who will tackle harder than anyone else, and those that would rather not play at all than pull out of a 50–50 ball. Then there was the apprentice Peter Southey, a left back whom I got to know very early on in my career at Tottenham. Peter joined the club as a teenager, and was a very elegant player, very skilful and fast. He quickly got picked for the reserves and before long he was chalking up many games, and being tipped for a position on the first team. He was one of those rare apprentices that you just knew would become a superstar.

But he kept complaining he was feeling tired, and for such a fit guy it was concerning. Peter grew very lethargic and began to struggle with training. We went through the obvious things, and the doctor ran tests to find out if he was anaemic, but when they got the results back the answer was something much more terrible. At 19, they diagnosed Peter with cancer, and told him he'd never play for Spurs again. His career was instantly over, and it was devastating for Peter and everyone who knew him. There was an atmosphere of sadness for a long while, and I remember they gave him jobs in various parts of the clubs, doing desk jobs. He loved the club so much he wanted to continue in any capacity, all the while battling this terrible cancer.

Which he did, until finally he died in 1984. There was a testimonial for him against Fulham that year, and, to me, he remains one of Tottenham's toughest fighters. It's criminal that a lad with so much promise should be struck down with a disease that wrecked a career before it started.

CHAPTER 14
CHAIRMEN OF THE BOARD

When I first started at Spurs, you never saw the chairman around the club, and certainly not any of the board members. At that time, in the Seventies, the chairman's name was Arthur Richardson, and, together with a family called the Webbs, they had control of the business side of Tottenham Hotspur for many years. Like many chairmen they had other businesses, and it seemed like the principle reason that Richardson or the board would be seen at the club was for board meetings. They were quite elderly, I seem to remember, and I didn't really know anything about them. I didn't know whether or not they had any football knowledge, or even if they were Spurs fans as kids.

As a keen as mustard groundsman, I used to speak to the other staff and ask lots of questions. I was told that the chairman and his board 'keep themselves to themselves and that's the way we like it'. It always seemed bizarre to me that a person in charge of such a massive operation would have such sparse experience of how the club was run at grass-roots level. That was all about to change.

In 1982, the club was acquired by a man called Irving Scholar, and everything changed. Scholar wrestled control from the Richardson and Webb families, who had owned the club for decades. He reportedly had the idea of buying the club while en route to watch Spurs play away at Leeds – which meant that he was both a serious fan and a crazy one, not just to be travelling the country watching away fixtures, but considering buying a football club during a particularly turbulent era for the British economy.

Irving was, of course, a massive Spurs supporter, which in my eyes is the very minimum requirement for a chairman, but fortunately I'm not in charge of picking them. Irving would become a very important part of not only Tottenham Hotspur, but also the story of football history in England. Of course, today you see many chairmen who are fanatical supporters of their clubs, such as Newcastle United's millionaire owner Mike Ashley. The proprietor of various successful sports shop chains, he can often be spotted in the crowd with travelling away fans, wearing a replica shirt and downing pints of lager!

But back then, it was the first time I'd ever seen or

heard of a chairman taking over a football club of which he was a fanatical supporter. Irving didn't waste any time in getting stuck in. He played for Spurs at White Hart Lane in a charity match, when a few better-off supporters bid at an auction to play for a legends team. And of all the people who had paid through the nose for the chance to run out at White Hart Lane, the happiest, most excitable player on the pitch was Irving Scholar, who was living his dream.

I played in that game, and Irving really got stuck in. It was a game prior to Ossie's testimonial, and I watched him run around, enjoying every moment, savouring every pass. Irving later played a charity game at Leyton Orient's Brisbane Road, hooked on the buzz of pulling on that famous lily-white shirt, but he got so involved in that game that he suffered quite a nasty injury.

The ball was played to me on the left side of midfield, and Irving was playing up front. I pushed the ball on to him, for him to run on to. How strange, I recall thinking, the most important man at the club playing alongside lowly staff members! But as he turned to chase after my pass, I heard a massive snap, and Mr Chairman hit the deck, screaming, 'Who kicked me?!' He was writhing in agony on the floor, and I remember thinking, 'This doesn't look good.' But there was no one around him. He shouted again, 'Who tackled me like that?!' but there was no one within ten metres of him. He'd ruptured his Achilles tendon in the worst possible way. I watched as the chairman, in full Spurs kit, was stretchered off the pitch in agony. 'Now that's dedication,' I thought. In the end he had to have an operation, and for the next few games I saw him arrive at White Hart Lane in a wheelchair, still with his Spurs scarf on. He was a die-hard.

One of the best things about Irving was that you'd bump into him around the stadium and he'd say, 'Hello, Roy, how's life? What's going on in the club?' He loved the game. It was Irving who decided to float Spurs on the Stock Exchange. These were the giddy Eighties, when anything seemed possible, yet at the same time, no one in the country could predict that England was to suffer so badly in the 1990s. Spurs diversified into leisurewear and computer systems, one of the first clubs to really capitalise on sponsorship and kit deals. And it was all Irving's doing. But the stadium at White Hart Lane also needed a new stand, and the club needed new players. Tottenham Hotspur was growing at a terrifying pace.

During the mid-Nineties when the Sky money and the Champions League cash-cow seemed to make the very top clubs unbeatable investments, Irving was keen to try to make Spurs one of those top teams – but it was proving difficult. Working on the staff at Spurs, you never knew the financial ins and outs of the club, and it certainly didn't have anything to do with me at the time. But one of the few times I got involved directly with the chairman was when we had to choose the next year's kit.

Irving was deeply interested in choosing the kit and was fanatical about colourways, the away kit and even the colour of the socks. He knew before everyone else that the kits would become big business. We started to have a home kit that would last two years and an away kit for one, and Irving was very influential in how to market the away kits, and make supporters desire two kits instead of just one.

I always called chairmen 'Mr Chairman', because that's what you did at Tottenham Hotspur, and Irving Scholar certainly won the hearts and minds of the team and the staff. I don't know why Scholar eventually resigned – it was business and therefore nothing to do with me – but he made a point of making a speech to everyone before he left.

The next chairman was a man who had grown up in a council estate in Hackney, East London. A man who had left school at 16 to sell car aerials and electrical goods out of a van he had bought with his savings. He was of course Sir Alan Sugar, one of the most successful entrepreneurs of his generation and soon to be one of the most important men in the history of Tottenham Hotspur Football Club.

What you see is what you get with Sir Alan. There are no airs and graces, and if he didn't like something he'd tell you, without hesitation. People who know me and know that I worked for Sir Alan always ask me what he's like in real life, having seen him on the TV show *The Apprentice*. They watch the show and say to me, 'That must all be for the cameras!' Well, perhaps the bit where he growls, 'You're fired' is put on (although no doubt he did utter that phrase to a few souls at the club in his time). When you see him talking to the new prospects, and he tells them how it is, he can be cutting: he's so abrupt, but he's always right. Sir Alan doesn't pull the wool over your eyes; if there's a problem, he addresses it. If you're not doing something right, he will tell you in his own way what the problem is, and at least you know where you stand. For that, I had nothing but admiration for him,

When I worked with my dad's furniture firm all those years ago, I found the foreman and the bosses so phoney and false. The foreman would get someone else to come and give you criticism, or you'd be lied to, but, with Sir Alan, you'd get it from the horse's mouth. I really respected the way he'd come from nothing, how he grew up poor and started his computer empire from absolutely nothing. A lot of the players respected him, because he was one of them. He'd grown up on an estate like many of them.

After a takeover battle with Robert Maxwell, Sir Alan teamed up with Terry Venables and bought Tottenham Hotspur Football Club in June 1991. But for some reason Sir Alan was not popular with some sections of Spurs' passionate supporters, and some accused him of having little knowledge of the football side of things. In his nine years as chairman, Spurs did not finish in the top six in the league and won just one trophy, the 1999

Worthington Cup, but I suppose his most unpopular move was to sack Terry Venables the night before the FA Cup Final, a decision which led to Venables appealing to the High Court to get himself reinstated. An ugly legal battle for the club took place over the summer, which Sir Alan won, but he later admitted that he felt 'as though I'd killed Bambi'.

Although a multi-millionaire, Sir Alan would never walk past you in the corridor at Spurs. He'd always say, 'Hello, Roy. Things well? Good, good.' He was a lot more brisk than Irving Scholar. He was a busy bloke. One afternoon, when we'd just signed with Adidas and the team were about to fly off on a pre-season tour, the Adidas delivery had just arrived at the training ground, and I was laying out the hundreds of pieces of training wear, ready for it to be loaded into skips. Suddenly Sir Alan walked in, and let me tell you, if you've never been in the same room as the guy, you certainly knew when he was around – he had such an important aura. Anyway, there was about £20,000 worth of unmarked, top Adidas training gear in the room, brand new, with labels on, and I was knee-deep in it on my own, separating everything into the right sizes for the players.

'Morning,' said Sir Alan, in his normal abrupt manner. 'What's all this then?'

I explained that I was preparing for the tour.

'Looks all right, doesn't it?' he replied, picking up a T-shirt and holding it up like he was inspecting it on one of those market stalls where he had started his career. Now, Sir Alan is a very keen tennis player. He's got a dangerous serve, so I'm told. And he clearly fancied some of the new tennis kit.

'What size are these?' he asked, rummaging through like he was at a jumble sale. 'Got any socks?'

And so the millionaire went around, picking up a few sets, all in his size. Then he just walked out. I was laughing, because it was so funny watching Sir Alan 'shopping'. He turned around at the doorway and laughed, 'Right, I'm having this lot, and if you don't like it, take it out my wages!' And with a smile, he was gone. It was brilliant, the way he did it. As if he got wages... he owned the place!

And that was the key to being a successful chairman, in my experience – being the top man at the club, enjoying a bit of banter with someone right at the bottom. Like Irving Scholar playing in the team for a charity match, Sir Alan knew the importance of knowing what was going on – from the socks to the signing of megastars.

In 1994, Sir Alan financed the transfers of three stars from the 1994 World Cup: Romanians Ilie Dumitrescu and Gica Popescu, and, most notably, Jürgen Klinsmann. While manager Ossie Ardiles commanded the media spotlight by pursuing various Brazilians, Sir Alan moored his yacht off Monte Carlo for negotiations with Klinsmann. No International footballer was more disliked in England than the 'golden bomber' before his arrival on these shores in August 1994. Jürgen had played in the West German side that beat England in the semi-final of the World Cup in 1990, then went on to have Argentina's Pedro Monzon sent off in the final and also win a penalty by seemingly making a meal of a questionable challenge. He wasn't flavour of the month. But somehow, Sir Alan was to attract a superstar with the power to change everyone's opinion of him.

Jürgen notched up five goals during Germany's bumpy run to the World Cup quarter-finals in 1994. He had attracted interest from Sampdoria and two Spanish clubs, but it was the personal touch from Sir Alan that lured the German to White Hart Lane. No one really knows how he did it, but, when he had the German's signature on paper, the bookmakers who were quoting Ardiles' side as 125–1 for the Premiership slashed their odds to 50–1.

It wasn't just Jürgen who enjoyed the hospitality of *Mein Host* Sir Alan onboard '*HMS Amstrad*'. That Christmas, myself and the other members of the staff were given instructions to attend a special Christmas meal, with no other information than to meet at London Bridge Station in the City of London. No one knew where we were going, but we were met by Sir Alan, who had arranged a special lunch on board his yacht, which he'd moored up on the Thames. It was a fantastic gesture, and a real treat. Whether you were the World Cup-winning striker whose signature he was chasing, or the kit man, he would treat you the same and you were welcome on his boat.

Sir Alan was there, holding court, and the food was sublime; we had the best turkey I've ever eaten. Sir Alan's assistant at the time was called Claude Littner, and he was great company. Claude had become chairman and chief executive of Amstrad International in the early 1990s, and then chief executive of Tottenham Hotspur for six years from 1993, and was the eyes and ears of Sir Alan at the club. It was to become an interesting time, and Sir Alan's signings were to quickly become Tottenham Hotspur legends.

Klinsmann had a remarkable first season, being crowned Footballer of the Year – the ultimate accolade in English football. However, because Spurs had not qualified for the UEFA Cup, Klinsmann decided to invoke an opt-out clause in his contract and left for Bayern Munich in the summer of 1995, which was a horrible shock for everyone, including Sir Alan. The chairman famously appeared on television holding the last shirt Klinsmann ever wore for Spurs and said he wouldn't even wash his car with it. He then labelled foreigners coming into the Premier League on high wages as 'Carlos Kickaballs', which was hilarious, really. The whole episode goes to show how far the role of chairman had come in such a short time. I worked at the club for years and never met Chairman Richardson. That day I watched Sir Alan on television speaking his mind about the departure of our best striker, football was becoming more transparent, and all the better for it, if you ask me.

I still believe Sir Alan always had Spurs' interests at heart. He always believed his decisions would help the club, even though the fans didn't see that every time. It's difficult for me to say this, because I was on the inside looking out, but I think it's far too easy for a fan to get disgruntled with results. I would be in the stadium after a poor result at home, loading the skips into the van, and there'd be a lynch mob outside on Bill Nicholson Way, chanting, 'Get the chairman out!' but you'd never hear them calling for a striker to be sold. You'd have a thousand people shouting, 'Sugar out!' and it makes a lot of noise outside the front gate, but I don't think that's the best thing for the club.

As far as Sir Alan was concerned, you could tell that even when he made mistakes – even when he got angry with Jürgen Klinsmann and threw that shirt at the reporter – he was passionate about his club. That day I saw a man so bitterly disappointed that Jürgen couldn't be part of the team he was helping to build, and, for that, Sir Alan was just like you or me. Even towards the latter part of his reign as chairman, even when there were confrontations with fans, Sir Alan would be at every game. Like Irving Scholar before him, Sir Alan never missed a game and was always there with his Spurs scarf on.

In February 2001, he sold his majority stake in Tottenham Hotspur to leisure group ENIC, selling his

27% share of the club for £22 million. Then, finally in June 2007, Sir Alan sold his remaining shares to ENIC for £25 million, ending his 16-year association with the club. And the proof of the pudding about Sir Alan's dedication for the club? I still see him at home games today.

I knew Daniel Levy meant business as soon as he arrived at White Hart Lane, mainly because he arrived with a removal van. Daniel Levy moved his office into White Hart Lane, bringing with him his wife, Tracey. Daniel was unlike Sir Alan, a completely different personality, perhaps a touch more approachable. Straight away, Mr Levy showed a great interest in the kits, which gave us some common ground. He and Tracey scrutinised sketches of next year's kits for hours, making sure they made the right choice. He was involved in bringing in Italian super-brand Kappa as our kit sponsor, which was rather brave, as no English team had ventured down that particular road. He even flew me, the club secretary and the commercial manager to Kappa's headquarters in Turin to look at samples. We were to see the new product to make sure it was OK, because Italian sizes were different to our own. We pored over swatches of materials and size charts, making sure everything was just right. I remember thinking, 'Now this is an exceptional level of detail.'

If you weren't happy with something, Daniel Levy would sort it out. If there was a kit issue, particularly with the negotiations with a new manufacturer, you could always go to him and he'd tell you what was going on. When I spoke to other kit men at other clubs, they'd tell me they'd never met their chairmen, and I know how that feels. But Levy was different, and today, when I hear about Daniel Levy travelling to Croatia to hold talks with Luka Modric and getting him to sign for another six years, I think that is how a chairman should be. Perhaps he's got a bit of the Sir Alan about him, as he'll travel the world for Tottenham Hotspur. He's been at the club just nine years, and we're playing Champions League football, we're finishing at the top of the league, and there's a new training ground in the pipeline – and a new stadium, to boot.

The appointment of a new management team, including the highly regarded Juande Ramos as head coach, resulted in our first trophy in nine years, when, on 24 February 2008, Spurs beat Chelsea 2–1 at Wembley in the Football League Cup Final. It also meant qualification for the UEFA Cup. But often, with chairmen, the grass is always greener on the other side. So next time the results don't go your way, think before you start chanting outside the main gates. Tottenham Hotspur is a club that has never had problems like the Glazers at Manchester United. Levy's plans for a new stadium include leisure areas, public spaces, a museum, restaurants, shops and apartments. Like Scholar and Sir Alan before him, Daniel Levy sees Spurs as a top-four club.

CHAPTER 15

SCORING FOR SPURS

When you read footballers' autobiographies, they often claim they were born to play the game. Well, I feel the same. My earliest memories were dreaming of playing for my team, Tottenham Hotspur. I yearned to tear down the left wing, embarrass a couple of defenders and break the net off the goal in front of the Paxton End with an outrageous strike, in a heated victory against our rivals, Arsenal. In my mind, my life was destined to become some kind of dramatic *Roy of the Rovers* finale. But, as you've already read, these dreams were shattered at the age of 12, when I was released by Tottenham.

But, like many things, it's not over till the fat lady sings, and my football days were far from over. As I progressed through the ranks of the backroom staff of Tottenham Hotspur, I always got stuck in to staff games

195

behind the scenes at the club, and loved every kick and tackle. It's a little-known fact that there was a ball court upstairs above the stadium building that was used for training the team when the training pitches were unavailable. In the early 1980s, still with a decent left foot and always itching for a game, I used to play in hastily organised seven-a-side matches that would kick off every Monday night on that ball court, and would continue to be played there for over a decade.

Groundsman Andy Church would invite some of his mates, the rest of the backroom staff would join in, and we'd be 15-strong, with rolling subs: living out our artificial dreams on an artificial football pitch just yards from the real thing. After a few years, we'd made up quite a decent side, and soon we took to inviting local sides in the area to come and play us, many of whom we would despatch in glorious style. The senior players would often come and watch, and occasionally, when numbers dwindled, you'd get the odd first-team player turning out. You should have seen the look on the faces of one team of civil servants who turned up to find that they'd be marking Paul Gascoigne!

We'd look forward to Monday nights religiously – it was a chance for us backroom boys to show what we could do. Afterwards, we'd have a shower and walk over to the White Hart pub and have a beer or an orange juice with the opposition, before slipping off home. Some of my happiest memories at Spurs happened on that ball court.

Years later, Stevie Perryman and a few of the ex-players boys formed an ex-Spurs team, and he asked me if I fancied a game. Fancy a game? Of course I would! And so I was selected to play at big games for the Ex-Spurs XI – like the annual match at the Chigwell police ground, where we'd play an Ex-Arsenal team. There I was, turning out for Spurs against Arsenal, in front of up to 600 fans. You see, sometimes, in a roundabout way, dreams can come true. These little North London derbies certainly got lively; sometimes at these clashes you'd be grateful there were so many coppers around! But of course the main aim was to earn a nice few quid for a charity, and hundreds, sometimes thousands, would turn out to watch the likes of Martin Chivers, Micky Hazard, Steve Grenfell and Pat Jennings. For the ex-players it was all a nice opportunity to have a run-out and relive their old memories, but for me it was a dream come true to play with these stars.

John Pratt used to play regularly, and he was a loony! One time, at Old Owens in Potters Bar, John decided he'd play in goal. He told us before we kicked off, 'Here, lads, I'm not going to use my hands for the entire game!' We said, 'You're mad, John,' but watched as he took to the field and managed to save everything kicked at him with his feet, head and even his arse! Fair play to him, he got everything, even chesting down shots and volleying them away. One ball flew into the box very high, and the opposition were clearly not amused by this performance, and, as John came out to head the ball, someone absolutely clattered him. He was unconscious before he hit the ground! I suppose it served him right, but in a way it was really funny and I think he saw the funny side when he finally came round!

We had some great games for the Ex-Spurs XI: I played with Graham Roberts and Ossie Ardiles against a Parliament XI and there's a great picture of me and Ossie tackling each other... a battle of the mighty midgets! I even played with Ricky Villa and Irving Scholar in another match, so I took to the pitch with some of Tottenham Hotspur's greatest ever players and even its chairman. Not bad for a boy from Edmonton with modest ability.

Every Spurs fan there's ever been has dreamed of playing at White Hart Lane, and I was no different. Since I was a little lad I used to stand on the terraces, with my brother-in-law Roger, and watch Tottenham Hotspur do battle under those floodlights. As a kid I would look wistfully at that bronze cockerel above the West Stand, and ponder whether I would become one of the cherished few who would get to run out on to that lush pitch wearing a lily-white shirt... to be one of the glorious 11 to represent Tottenham Hotspur, to proudly play for the team I adored. Bizarrely, it would only take me a few years working at Spurs before I would achieve that dream.

On 29 April 1980, Spurs legend Terry Naylor's testimonial was played against a Crystal Palace team at

White Hart Lane. Tough-tackling Naylor had featured in both legs of the 1974 UEFA Cup Final against Feyenoord and was an unused substitute in both legs of the 1972 UEFA Cup Final against Wolverhampton Wanderers FC. He had played 243 games for Tottenham Hotspur. Terry's testimonial would be a fitting end to a fine career, but I was shocked and surprised when Terry came up to me on the morning of the match and said, 'Do you fancy a game, Roysie?' Well, I was working on the ground staff at the time, and I suppose Terry knew I could play from watching the ball court games on a Monday night. Of course, I jumped at the chance.

In truth, they were probably struggling for numbers, but either way, I was in the team, to play in an exhibition match before the main game at 6.30pm, and my knees, like in Ossie's famous song, had gone all trembly. I remember we got changed in the junior dressing rooms next to the players' lounge and we walked through the car park with our studs clattering on the concrete, and out of the old tunnel. This was particularly magical for me, as this was how the team used to run out when I stood as a kid, watching with Roger. As the team filed out on to the pitch and the din of the large crowd rose into a full-blown cheer, I thought of Roger, and those days we'd stand on the terraces. He would be taking bets with the opposition fans, while I watched on, hypnotised by those beautiful white shirts pouring on to the pitch. Today, it was my turn.

The pitch was like a bowling green. The fact I'd worked on it for Bill Nicholson made it seem strange for me to be playing on it, instead of yelling at people to get off the grass! The bright-green turf was perfectly manicured, the blades short, stout and wet. They'd sprinkled it, and the glossy surface was sheer perfection. When we warmed up, I rolled the ball to another player with no pace on it, and the grass actually moved the ball – every time it rolled over a section of the grass that was rolled in one direction, it would gently tug the ball left and right. It was poetic. The ball would whir and sing as it zipped across the grass! I couldn't stop smiling.

They kicked off and I remember sighing and saying how great the pitch was. Mark Kendall, the Welsh goalkeeper played in goal for us, and, as I slipped off my training top and put on the lily-white shirt, a number 15, for the first time, a shiver danced down my spine. I ran on, to play on the left behind Jimmy Greaves. I briefly recalled that day I chased after his car on the High Road, and how I politely asked for his autograph. When I got my chance to go on as a second-half substitute, it was like playing on sponge: every pass you hit, every pass you received went so true, it arrived perfectly at your feet. Now, I was used to playing on the lumpy and bumpy pitches of Sunday-league football and, let me tell you, playing at White Hart Lane was like playing a different sport. It was like every dream I'd ever had set here at White Hart Lane.

There must have been a good 10,000 in the crowd, which was nerve-wracking. Our opposition were a team of businessmen and fans who had paid a lot of money to play against us, but I remember hoping that the game wouldn't end like my last run-out at White Hart Lane, a staff game on the pitch, which had ended tragically. One afternoon we'd played a match behind closed doors – backroom staff versus match-day staff – and there was a big security guard called Terry playing in defence for them. Somehow, I ended up at centre forward, and, as the ball got rolled towards him, Terry ran back towards his own goal with it. I was chasing him up, and for some reason he decided to turn and try to go round me, but I tackled him. It was a pretty straightforward tackle, but Terry went down in a terrible heap, screaming, 'You've broken my legs!'

We played on, and I thought nothing of it, but, as the ball was played down the pitch, I noticed he was still down. I thought, 'This doesn't look good.' And indeed, when they examined him in hospital, he had broken both of his legs. It was a complete accident: Terry had turned awkwardly, and anyone who's ever been tackled by me knows I'm no 'Nutty' Naylor. But I was very sad for the security guard and later visited him in hospital.

Back on the pitch at White Hart Lane, I was so proud to be back and playing. There were some good ex-pros in that team, including Cliff Jones, who was capped 59 times for Wales and was a crucial member of Tottenham Hotspur's 1960/61 Double-winning side. Cliff was at the time widely considered as the best left-winger in the world, and I was playing just behind him. I'd collected his autograph too as a child. I was buzzing – absolutely high on adrenaline and boyish excitement.

I watched Cliff pick up the ball and cut into the left-hand side of the box, and, as he went to go round a defender, he was blocked. The crowd stood up as the ball ran loose to the edge of the box, zipping along that fast turf beautifully into my path. I don't know why I hit it really. I bet Steve Perryman would have shouted at me to play it simple, if it hadn't gone where it did.

The ball bent like a dream and hit the post before clinking round the back of the net, and I watched as the smattering of supporters jumped up. It was a glorious goal. When I scored I felt like taking the shirt off and never playing again. It was a great feeling, but I resisted celebrating: I remember feeling embarrassed! Cliff Jones embraced me, and over his shoulder I looked up to where I used to stand as a kid, imagining a younger me staring down at this scene. I could have cried.

But of course I had to sort out all the kit afterwards, which took the edge off it. Two lots of extra kits that weekend! Bloody hell!

I suppose the greatest honour for me was being able to play with Stevie Perryman, my all-time Spurs hero. But I remember it was no easy ride! Stevie had a go at me once, which really hurt. He had laid the ball off to me, and instead of playing the way I was facing, as was the Spurs way at the time, I played it away blind, a bit of a fancy pass that failed to come off. Even though we were playing a team of overweight, panting businessman who'd paid a couple of grand to have a kick-around, Perryman yelled at me, 'Play it simple, for fuck's sake!' I was just glad to be there I suppose. But that was Stevie: even in those kick-abouts he didn't want to get beaten. Martin Chivers would play like that too, and he was no spring chicken, even then. But I'd be busting a gut to keep up and Martin and Stevie would be coasting. Players like Gary Brook would be 30 yards from goal, line one up with no back-lift, and it would take the net off. Tony Galvin would drop that shoulder of his and completely bamboozle two defenders, and he'd stroll past them both. That's the difference between professional players and the likes of me, and noticing that helped me come to terms with the fact that I never made it as a player.

But as one of the millions who never 'made it', I count myself lucky to have in my memory a goal scored at White Hart Lane. Players have served their club for years and not got there, even some like Steffen Freund, who made it into the Tottenham Hotspur Hall of Fame and never got on the score sheet. After the testimonial, I went back to my house in Bruce Grove and I immediately called my sister to tell her and Roger about my goal. I desperately wished Roger could have seen me score, because he would have got one hell of a kick out of it. My sister picked up the phone, and the first thing she said was, 'What a goal!'

I couldn't believe it! She and Roger had been right there, behind the goal, with their daughter Julie, and saw the moment I scored for Tottenham Hotspur. They had no idea I was playing (if I'd have known, I would have rung everyone I'd ever met and they would have had a full house at the Lane that day) but they'd turned up on the spur of the moment, and were as surprised as I was to see me pop up and score a 30-yard strike! Sadly, it was to be one of the last games Roger saw at White Hart Lane, for he passed away soon after that. He was only 39, a victim of Huntingdon's disease, a tragic, hereditary disease that would later claim the life of his son at a similarly young age.

But life goes on, and I played on, and was included in many other big games, including one that I suppose was one of the highlights of my career at Tottenham Hotspur. There was a Spurs charity game at Cheshunt against a team of Norwegian internationals who turned out in a bright fluorescent-pink kit. They were called 'The Horribles', and the game was organised by Stevie Perryman, who used to be involved with the Norwegian team Burgen. I was up for it, as always, still proud to pull on that white shirt, and still dreaming of scoring goals for Spurs.

We turned up on the Sunday, and all I knew was Andy Church was in goal, and Peter Shreeves, who was then assistant manager, was playing too. But as we got changed, all of a sudden, England's Martin Peters walked into the dressing room. I remember thinking, 'This is really something.' Then Peter Taylor arrived, and then John Pratt. When Bobby Moore opened the door, I nearly fell over. 'Hold on a minute,' I thought, 'I'm in a team here with two World Cup winners.' I could feel my heart beating faster, but as I pulled the jersey over my head, I looked up and saw George Best. It took my breath away. George Best!

I had grown up watching George Best; he was a left-sided player and I admired him greatly. On that occasion I remember George walking into the dressing room with a big bushy beard and long hair, and he looked like a rock star. Perryman had told me there'd be a few surprises, but this team was something else: Chivers, Moore, Peters, Best... I mean, when people talk about legends and superstars, this lot were top of the tree. When they read out the team sheet, and my name was included, I felt a bit faint. They called Martin Peters 'The Ghost' because he would arrive late, like a spirit at the back post. Playing with these guys was weird, even calling their names! 'George! Martin!' I would remember this experience for the rest of my life.

For some reason I played on the right, with George Best behind me. I would have played in goal, anywhere, to be on this team. George said to me as we strolled out, 'Come and play on the right, I'll play behind you, and I'll make you look a good player.' I'll never forget it. Now, I'm a left-sided player, and I was frankly shitting it, playing with George Best on my 'wrong' side. But every time he'd get the ball, Best would do a trick and play it to me. He'd do another trick, and play it to me. And with the ball, he'd say to me, 'Control it, look up, if it's not on, give it back.'

We went through the whole game like that, and I never put a foot wrong. George Best told me what to do, when and how, and I followed every word. Then, with minutes left to go, we had a corner on the right-hand side. Best picked up the ball to take it, and said to me, 'They're all going to be in the six-yard box marking each other, so just stand on the edge of the box, and run towards the penalty spot when I make my run.'

Now, I'm 5'6" with studs on, so no one bothered to mark me, and when Best crossed this ball it was like he'd measured it. I ran on to the penalty spot and the ball was so perfectly weighted I didn't need to leave the floor. I thought, 'If this goes in, I'm going to pack up playing and never kick a ball again.' The ball hit my head with pinpoint precision, and I didn't have to jump more than half a foot off the floor to meet it. The sweat was dripping off me after 90 minutes trying to keep up with Georgie Best, and I remember the sound the ball made when it hit my forehead with a slap. It was just a really weird feeling. Have you ever had one of those dreams where you're being chased and you can't run? I watched the ball fly into the top corner and the keeper didn't even move for it. I wanted to do handstands, a Roger Miller dance around the corner flag, a Jose Dominguez summersault, and the works. But I managed to keep myself under control and as I jogged back to the halfway line Georgie Best shook my hand, and said just this: 'Told you.'

It was the happiest day of my life, to be on the pitch with that calibre of player, with a man that had picked up the Jules Rimet trophy for England, Moore, George Best and Steve Perryman! It was a schoolboy dream come true. During the taking of the team photo before the game, I remember being like a little boy; I was a running up to the photographer saying, 'Can I have one of those?... You won't forget, will you?' After the game, I again begged him, 'You won't forget, will you?' For a week afterwards I was telling my mates about the game I'd played with George Best and the goal I scored, and they didn't know whether to believe me.

I don't think I would have believed me either, but when the photograph came through I took it round to show a few of my mates, and when I saw the look on their faces it was brilliant. Years later, John Pratt gave me the same team photo as a present, framed, and signed on the back. For all the important items that have meant things to me in sport, from schoolboy medals to amateur cup final medals, that photograph is my most prized possession. I would run back into a burning house to save that picture. I'm smiling out of that photograph like the little boy who used to stand at White Hart Lane watching his heroes on a Saturday afternoon. I used to love it when George Best came to the Lane, because he was more than just a great player. The sports cars and the women, the haircuts and the step-overs and the epic goals – there were so many similarities between George and Gazza, many of which would be revealed after their careers ended. They both had phenomenal power, but with those strengths came destructive weaknesses... troubles that would later be the death of George Best, in November 2005.

CHAPTER 16
IT'S A HARD LIFE

On the bench at White Hart Lane, we used to get through up to 20 packets of chewing gum in 90 minutes. Sometimes more, in cup games. On my way to the ground, I used to stop at the same sweet shop and buy an entire box of Wrigley's, which would be angrily, urgently and joyously chewed away by jaws clenched tightly with nervous energy. Chomping on that gum was the only release from the endless stress of life on the sidelines, which I can only explain by taking you along with me, on a typically emotional day of my life.

I've chosen an FA Cup fourth-round clash with Manchester City, and you can join me for every kick of the game, and chew over every detail of a gruelling match day at one of the most exciting football clubs in the world. I'll take you where normal fans aren't allowed to go, behind the closed doors of the dressing room, and alongside me on the bench. Let me take you back to Wednesday, 4 February 2004. Big-boned singer Michelle McManus is at number one in the charts with 'All This Time', and serial killer Dr Harold Shipman has just been found hanged in his cell. Spurs have arrived in the fourth round of the FA Cup having dismantled Crystal Palace 3–0, and previously beaten the same Manchester City side 3–1 in the League Cup just weeks before.

David Pleat is caretaker manager of Spurs, after Glenn Hoddle was dismissed after a cruel defeat to his former club, Southampton. Striker Jermain Defoe has just signed for us, but will be unable to play in this clash that we are expected to win, at all costs. Typically, northerly winds are battering London and it's freezing cold, but I never wear a coat to work. It's concentration, mainly: I'm too busy to be cold. I'm nervous the moment I arrive at White Hart Lane, much like the players, who are filtering in to the dressing room, each of them smartly dressed in collar and tie. It's 12.30pm and the referees are upstairs enjoying a lunch of chicken and pasta. I'm downstairs in the dressing room, laying out the kit.

'Have you got my size medium shorts?' comes a lilting Irish voice behind me, as I lay out some Marks and Spencer sandwiches on the table. It's Robbie Keane, immaculately turned out as usual.

'Yes Rob,' I sigh. 'Same size you've had for the last 27 games.'

Robbie peeps inside the shorts, and playfully taps me

on the shoulder. 'Top man, Roysie,' he says, and loosens the knot in his blue tie.

Helder Postiga is fingering his shirt on the hanger, checking the size is right. 'You got my new socks, Roysie?' he asks with a smile.

I show him the plastic Kappa bag containing his brand-new socks, and without a word I lay out the large bags of Haribo sweets that the players have become accustomed to. Sweets are something I don't reckon Bill Nicholson would have approved of, but sports physiology has come a long way since the 1960s, and today's players understand the importance of a short spike in glucose levels before taking to the field.

'Hello, Kasey,' I say to our American goalkeeper. Kasey and the players are busy sorting out tickets for friends and relatives, as I pick up the media team sheets, which are always useful to me, as they have the line-ups of both teams. I scour down the list of names: City have Fowler up front, the former Liverpool striker and lethal goal machine, and young Wright-Phillips, a lad with frightening pace down the right-hand side. I look up from the team sheet and the dressing room is now full of the Spurs players on that list: Keller, Gardner, Ziege, Carr, Richards, King, Brown, Davies, Dalmat, Postiga, Keane and a bench full of subs. They're all shaking hands, dressed in posh designer suits and smelling of expensive colognes and fragrances, mixing with the unmistakable scent of muscle spray.

I've spent the last few hours laying out the room to

perfection, and I'm happy, but nervous. The shirts are hanging with the names and numbers facing out, and there's a folded towel, match slip, warm-up top and rain jacket laid neatly below each kit. The players are flicking through the match-day programmes and talking about the game ahead. 'Big game today, lads,' says Robbie, clapping his hands together loudly. Once the players are changed and out for a group warm-up, I'm in the staff room out the back of the dressing room with manager David Pleat, Clive Allen, Hans Segers, and the physios and the doctor. The staff is ten-handed with the masseur included; you'd be surprised at the number of match-day staff there are. David Pleat is busy fiddling with the radio, as I guess he'll be up in the gods watching the first half, while assistant manager Chris Hughton will be on the touchline, but they'll be in full radio contact.

'This is a big, big game,' David Pleat begins, addressing the team who have returned from the warm-up. It's five to three and the players are all wearing their match shirts, and are sat patiently listening to the boss.

'Possession is key, we beat them before by keeping the ball, so no silly passes and let's retain our shape at the back. It's essential we don't concede, so let's get out there and get an early goal.'

Players are all very different on match day. Ledley has gone into his shell, and sits quietly meditating, Keano is very vocal and enthusiastic, while Ziege doesn't say a word to anyone. You can smell the grass when the dressing-room door opens – it has just been cut, and the white lines are glowing and freshly painted – and the players begin to file out into the bright corridor.

This is when the lads are at their most nervous. While they're having the photos taken, and the handshakes and all that stuff, they're just itching to kick off, and so am I. I hear the whistle blow from inside the dressing room, and the massive cheer that goes up when Keane nudges the ball to Postiga and play commences. While I haven't missed a home or away game in 27 years, I rarely see a kick-off, as I'm in the dressing room putting away the dirty warm-up stuff. I have to prepare now for the half-time break, and busy myself laying out the Gatorade and waters, and some tea for those players with a tea fetish.

I have to get my trusty kit bag ready, too – the emergency equipment I take to the dugout with me. There are three brand-new spare balls, the blood shirts and blood shorts in case of a messy injury, spare socks, a pair of pliers, a stud of each size and laces. Anything can go wrong, and you don't want to be running back into the dressing room. It's not far, but the English game is so fast-paced that, if a player is on the sidelines for 30 seconds without a lace, anything can happen. It can cost you the game.

The crowd is already roaring when I run up and out of the tunnel, and a peek up at the mega screen tells me just three minutes have gone. Kevin Keegan nods at me as I walk towards the bench. He always remembers me, does Kevin. The crowd are rising to their feet as I take my seat on the cold bench. The ball runs out of play and

Brown takes the throw-in. I unwrap my first chewing gum and stick it into my mouth as King receives the ball and surges forward, playing the ball on the edge of the box towards Dalmat, who deftly back-heels it to Davies. Simon threads the ball back into Ledley's path who is juggernauting into the City penalty area, and picks up the ball with ease. I've only just sat down but suddenly Ledley turns back on to his left foot just inside the area and the crowd, like me, are on their feet! Ledders lets rip with a real curler, and bang! It's 1–0 and I'm jumping for joy.

'You just made it,' Jeff, the physio, says to me, as we embrace.

'1–0,' I sigh, relieved. 'Just the start we need.'

You see, when you go 1–0 up, the whole place just breathes a collective sigh of relief. Steven Carr is captain and wearing the armband in the absence of Jamie Redknapp, and is calling to the back four to tighten up and keep possession. I scan across the players to check all the kit is in order and nothing's missing, no errant Premiership badges or shinpads.

Our Portuguese forward Helder Postiga is pulling up already, and suddenly there might be a substitution. I'm back on my feet again, as I need to know that whoever is coming on is ready. I look to Poyet who is the natural replacement for Postiga. 'You got your pads and boots tied up?' I ask him quickly. He nods, his eyes on the manager, waiting for the call.

Chrissie Hughton is standing up on the edge of the

technical area, where he will remain for the rest of the game. He looks concerned. Postiga is hobbling round the pitch and I hear Chris on the radio to David Pleat. 'Gus?' I hear Chrissie say into the microphone. He presses the earpiece further into his ear, receiving confirmation from the heavens, and next Gus is tearing off his warm-up top. His pads are in and his boots tied up all ready, because I'd recently had to have words with a few of the substitutes for not being ready to play. In a league game earlier in the season, a player had gone down injured, like this, in the early minutes, and the sub was wearing flip-flops, and his shinpads were on the floor. I was apoplectic with rage.

'You've got to be ready to come on at the drop of a hat,' I told them sternly. 'Even the reserve goalkeeper. You never know what'll happen.' Often, you'll tell a player he's coming on, and he'll say, 'I need the toilet first.' Now, that's nerves, and I understand that. But Gus is a seasoned pro, and he's itching to get on.

Chris is yelling, 'Keep the ball, lads,' and 'Keep it short, keep it tight!'

He'll be yelling this for 90 minutes. 'When we lose possession, get behind the ball, get yourself set, two blocks of four,' is his battle cry.

You'll hear this call on a Sunday morning at your local park, but sometimes even Spurs need reminding of the simple stuff. Gus runs on with the instructions from the boss, and plays just behind Robbie Keane who's having a quiet game so far. We're 1–0 up with no possession and it's 15 minutes gone. I'm on my fourth stick of gum.

'Go on, Ledley!' I shout as King slides in to dispossess a City forward.

I tend to shout at the players, but only encouragement and never tactical advice – that's the manager's job. Some managers encourage staff to shout and help the lads through a sticky time. 'Unlucky, next time,' you call, or give them a little gee-up. It's hard to explain, but if you're in the crowd it's easy to be critical, but when you're on the bench it's a different game. You feel for them a lot more. You know they're trying. My time is before the game and at half-time, where I give a little encouragement. 'The fullback's breathing out of this arse,' I'll tell a striker, 'you've got him now,' and he might say, 'Yeah, he's finished, Roysie.' It helps them find that half-a-yard.

Postiga's hurt and after the once-over from the doctor he's now back on the bench. I hand him a heavy coat to keep him warm, and ask, 'You OK, Helder?'

'Hamstring,' he says, with a grimace. He sits down beside me and he smells of sweat, but I'm used to it.

On the pitch, Christian Ziege swings in a left-footed free-kick from outside of the area, and the keeper struggles to catch it. The crowd behind us rise to their feet and suddenly drop back down again. 'Fucking hell!' I hear about a hundred blokes cry behind me on the West Stand. 'Close!'

Next, Robbie Fowler breaks past Dean Richards and slices the ball past Keller, but mercifully it goes wide of the post. This is real FA Cup football, exciting end-to-end stuff and a real treat for the neutral. But I'm not a neutral, and my nerves are getting jangled already. My first packet of chewing gum has been decimated and I'm in the box for another, handing a couple of packs around the bench.

Simon Davies performs a Brazilian-style back-heel to Robbie Keane, which comes off marvellously, but Hughton is on his feet swearing and shouting. I see the spittle flying from his mouth as he shouts, 'Stop flicking and fannying!' – another of his classic phrases. Davies sprints past and pretends he doesn't hear. It's fantastic if it comes off, but devastating if it doesn't. Suddenly, Robbie darts away and chases a long ball from Carr, and he's tearing into the City area with aplomb, mobbed by three defenders. Robbie takes one touch and deftly flicks the ball over the keeper with the outside of his left boot, and I'm on my feet again! I'm punching the air as the crowd go absolutely bananas.

Two-nil! Robbie does the cartwheel celebration, probably ruining another pair of shorts, and shoots those pretend bullets into the West Stand. Brilliant! There's only 20 minutes gone, and we've hardly touched the ball. But, after two fantastic goals, who can complain?

Next, Stephen Carr picks up the ball and the crowd shout: 'Shoot!' even though he's 45 yards from goal. It'll take them a few more years to forget his screamer here, against Manchester United. I'll never forget it and neither will Stephen. He wisely passes to Dalmat who is fouled, and slides across the turf awkwardly, smearing deep mud across his shirt. 'That's the end of that one,' I quip to the physio. That shirt will end up in the bin, as the laundry girls will never get that stain out.

It's hard keeping up with the shirts that are ruined by soiling. The groundsmen put fertiliser on the pitch and it kills shirts when it mixes with the grass. It gets so deep into the fabric that you have to throw shirts away. The laundry girls used too much bleach on Teddy's shirt once, and turned the Kappa logo and Spurs logo pink! The boys on *Soccer AM* noticed and Teddy's pink shirt made it to the 'Third Eye' section on the show the next week, and of course everyone was asking me about it. Today we'll just give Dalmat a new shirt out of the packet at half-time.

Back on the pitch, 40 minutes have flown past, and Manchester City's Joey Barton clashes with Michael Brown and picks up a booking that he's clearly not happy with. Brown's a tough player and puts himself about, and, as the pair square up to each other, I hear Barton shout at Michael, 'You fucking knob!' He gets in Michael's face again. 'Fucking knob!'

But Barton's pulled away into the wall by his team-mates, and I'm up on my feet again, but this time I've got to get back into the dressing room to prepare for half-time. You only get 15 minutes, and, while that may feel like a long time when you're putting a bet on or queuing for a burger or a pint, it goes far too quickly for us. I sprint down the tunnel and into the dressing room. I jump up and flick on the television set in the corner, and watch the flickering screen as Ziege puts the ball down.

The Sky TV graphic tells me Christian is 26.6 yards outside the box, and I see Keane standing over it too. Both of them stare at the ball. But it's Ziege who sprints towards it. There's a slight delay from real life to the TV set, as the action is lost somewhere in a satellite hovering thousands of miles above the Earth, so I hear an almighty roar from the crowd outside, as Ziege strikes the ball on TV. I jump in the air, and scream with delight, just me on my own, and watch as the TV shows the ball bend over the keeper and into the net. The replay shows the crowd behind the goal going mental, and I'm still saying, 'Yes!' as I pour out the tea for the lads.

I pour ten small teas, make sure the Lucozade is out, and I bring out a little clothes rail with second shirts for the players who I know would change. Stevie Carr will want a long sleeve, Ziege will need another, and of course Dalmat, and suddenly the lads pour in, sweating, panting and wet. It's all gone off and Robbie Keane is saying to Stephen Carr, 'He's been sent off! Barton's been sent off!'

'What for?' I ask. 'I was watching on the telly, I didn't see anything!'

I peer out the door to see what's going on, and Kevin Keegan walks past me in the tunnel. He turns to his assistant and says, 'Where's the nearest job centre round here?' I don't know if he's joking or not.

We're 3–0 up with ten men playing against us, and I think, 'What could go wrong?' but evidently, with

Tottenham Hotspur, anything can happen. David Pleat gives the lads five minutes. The team are medically checked, then they get their drinks, Robbie's trying to talk but he's breathing so heavily no one can understand him.

David Pleat takes over and addresses the team. 'OK, lads, first, we're three-nil up, not a wonderful amount of possession, but they haven't hurt us.'

Chris Hughton behind him adds, 'That's right, we need to keep the ball. Tight, tight, tight.'

'Roysie, can I have another shirt?' Robbie asks, and hurls his wet one at me.

'Cheers, Rob!' I say, peeling the wet shirt off my face. I hand him a fresh one from the rail. He checks the size, smiles at me and slips it on. Already the shirt sticks to his sweating torso.

Chrissie gives a little team talk, as I run round helplessly trying to pick up the dirty shirts and bits of tape that litter the dressing-room floor. I'm already exhausted and I've got a sweat on that makes it look like I was playing on the left wing, not sat in the dugout.

'Make sure you keep it tight in the first ten minutes and make sure you don't give away any free-kicks around the area,' warns Hughton, as the players, somewhat refreshed, file out once again into the tunnel.

Straight from the kick-off, Ledley brings down Wright-Phillips from behind and Chris is fuming. 'No free-kicks near the area!' he reminds the defender, who nods towards the bench by way of an apology. We're all up on our feet and so is their bench, as one of the City coaches shouts at us, 'You're having a laugh! He should be booked for that!'

I shout back, 'It's a fucking man's game, calm down!' I like a bit of banter with the opposition bench. 'Calm down!' I shout again, as the City bench continue to protest.

Our defenders assemble a wall and you can hear Kasey Keller's Washington accent above every other noise in the stadium. He sounds like an American general ordering his troops, as he screams, 'Right! Left!' But Macken lofts the ball to Distin – completely unmarked at the back post – who firmly heads the ball past Keller into the empty net. It's 3–1, and the City fans have found their voice with a rendition of 'Blue Moon'.

I peel the wrapper off another chewing gum, and think to myself for a minute, 'They've got one goal; come on, lads, just keep possession of the ball for ten minutes and frustrate them. We're still two goals in front.'

'Keep your shape, lads,' I say under my breath.

Christian Ziege comes off and Johnnie Jackson peels off his training top and runs on to replace him. Suddenly, it's like the Alamo, and City are camped in our area. Chrissie Hughton is yelling so hard he's already losing his voice. A pot shot from Paul Bosvelt flies off Gardner and past Keller... 3–2! Now we're in trouble. I'm going to need more gum.

City have taken control of the possession again, and we've got a real FA Cup tie on our hands. We need another goal to make this comfortable, and Hughton is tearing his hair out on the sidelines. If you look at our firepower, with Robbie Keane up front, you still fancy us to get another, and as the 64th minute comes around I'm kicking and heading every ball. 'Come on, lads!' I shout on to the pitch, at no one in particular. You see, it can be frustrating being on the bench. It's your job, and you want them to do well, but the players are your mates, and you've got so much emotional investment in the game. Every fixture is like a World Cup Final, your nerves are that frayed.

It's 3–2, and I catch myself thinking, 'If it stays like this, I'll take it and we'll go on and play Manchester United in the semi.' But the Spurs fans are getting aggravated at how badly we're playing, and from behind me the negative comments are beginning to fly. Now, I personally think that Spurs fans are among the top away supporters in the country, as, when you go away from home, they'll sing for 90 minutes straight. But today it's the City fans in full voice and the Spurs fans are moaning. It's reflected in the team as heads go down, and some sloppy passes fail to come off.

'You all right, Christian?' I ask Ziege, who has just arrived back on the bench. 'Yeah. How long left?'

'Ten minutes,' I tell him, showing him my digital watch and handing him a chewing gum. One of the fans behind the dugout shouts out, 'Well played, Ziege,' and the German puts his hand up in recognition. He knows that winning over a Spurs crowd is easy. Running and running for 90 minutes is all they ask for. But it's now 75 minutes on the clock and we're officially struggling.

We're peppering their box with long balls, when Brown knocks it into the box long, and Robbie Keane heads it down to the corner of the net, and suddenly the whole bench is standing up... is this the winning goal to make it 4–2? No! The keeper sticks out a desperate hand and saves the day again. The ball is thrown back at us, quickly again.

'Come on, lads!' I yell on to the pitch. My nerves are shot to shreds, as I look over at the opposition bench and McManaman is stripping off. They're going for it. And back on the pitch, Shaun Wright-Phillips is through on goal, and suddenly it's one-on-one.

Eighty minutes. Goal. 3–3. Bloody Tottenham. I unwrap my last stick of gum and pop it into my mouth, chewing angrily. Spurs' FA Cup games always taste of peppermint for me. David Pleat is on the bench now and he is absolutely fuming. 'Possession! Possession! Possession!' he screams, the spit flying out of his mouth as he yells.

McManaman's on and he's giving it everything for the last ten minutes. Chrissie Hughton asks for another packet of gum and I toss one over. This might go to extra time so I need to prepare. I sprint into the dressing room and quickly get some drinks ready, as the players will urgently need fluids. The physio is ready to massage the calves, and I'll have to chip in as well, rubbing those aching muscles, to try to get another half-an-hour out of already exhausted players. I line up all the drinks by the dressing-room door, ready to run and get them when the whistle blows, and sprint back out to watch the last kicks of the game. One minute of normal play remains.

'Come on, you Spurs!' The crowd are singing. But from Tarnat's cross from the left, Macken's header loops over Keller and into the back of the net. Disaster. My head is in my hands on the bench and I get this horrible nauseous feeling. 4–3 to City and we've thrown away a 3–0 lead. Total devastation. It's injury time now, and there's no comeback. City spend the last few minutes booting the ball into row Z, and when the whistle blows some of the Spurs players drop to their knees in utter disbelief. 'This is going to be a shit weekend,' I think, 'and an even worse Monday morning for the debrief.'

'Unlucky, lads,' I say as Michael Brown storms off with a face like thunder. A defeat adds half-an-hour on to your day. The lads sit in the dressing room, wearing haunted expressions. They don't want to take the shirts off. They don't want to face anyone – the crowd or their friends and family in the players' lounge – or indeed anyone. Robbie Keane flings a shinpad against the wall in anger, and I quietly go and pick it up. I feel his pain. And I know there's nothing I can say.

All I can do is walk sombrely around the dressing room and take the boots away from the players' feet and from the floor, and brush the mud off. David Pleat sits motionless on a bench as I take a handful of boots back to the kit room and start work. The boots are hot in my hands, warm with sweat. Sometimes, you even see steam rising out of the boots, as I wipe them over. I scrub them a little more angrily than I would if we had won. Spurs are out of the FA Cup, a competition we are famed for winning. With no cup run to look forward to, the fans are bitterly disappointed, and I don't relish tuning in my car radio to Radio 5 Live to listen to their thoughts.

Later, I skulk slowly into the car park, where a group of fans are peering through the gates. 'Fucking hell!' one of them shouts at me. 'How the hell did you lot throw that away?' The supporter is drunk and he's a few pints worse for wear, so I ignore him and open the car door. 'Wanker,' he shouts, as I slam the car door shut. I don't understand sometimes. Sure, I'm part of the team, but how can this be my fault? What's more, I love this team as much as, if not more than, this supporter. I understand this pain. I've seen it etched on the players' faces for the last hour as I saw them struggle to comprehend the loss. What's more, I've experienced more of these tragic losses than this supporter ever will, even if he goes to every home game for a few decades.

They should show the video of this game to younger, potential fans as a warning of how Spurs are famous for throwing away great leads, and to advise them not to start celebrating victories until we're at least 7–0 up and in injury time. For me, though, White Hart Lane is my place of work, and today is just another bad day at the office. I start the car. I'll be at the training ground tomorrow, washing the smell of defeat out of those shirts, for, like the players, the shirts will be fit to fight another day.

CHAPTER 17
FAREWELL, BILL NICHOLSON

Saturday afternoon, 23 October 2004, and White Hart Lane was deathly quiet. You could have heard a pin drop on the Shelf side, and only the gentle flutter of the corner flags replaced the usual cacophony of cheering and hollering that was commonplace for this particular corner of North London on match day. But, as Tottenham Hotspur and Bolton lined up on the wet grass of White Hart Lane, and the sun glared off the golden cockerel above us, the referee's shrill peep on the whistle ended the minute's silence in honour of William Edward 'Bill' Nicholson OBE. The club's greatest legend had died, aged 85, after a long illness, at a Hertfordshire hospital. And for 60 seconds the crowd had fallen silent in respect.

Nicholson had, of course, guided Spurs to the first League and Cup Double of the 20th century, having taken over as manager in 1958. His influence on the club, and me, was of epic proportions. I first met 'Mr Nicholson', as he always was to me, while hanging around outside the stadium, just off Tottenham High Road, N17, as a child, collecting autographs. The short road leading to the gates was an unnamed road back then, and often the manager would simply stroll out of the ground, whistling as he walked. Bill lived just minutes away on Crayton Road, and quite often you'd see him strolling down the road – and as such, for a committed autograph hunter like me, his signature was a relatively easy, yet satisfying acquisition.

Bill Nicholson was so approachable, and I seem to remember not very tall, which gave me a lot of hope in the days that I had dreamed of becoming a Spurs player myself. Bill was very polite and always had a lot of time for kids like me. I'd ask him, 'Mr Nicholson, may I please have your autograph?' and he'd always stop and make sure he could sign it properly, not like today's players who will scrawl anything on a photograph or shirt. I was enamoured by Bill Nicholson's handwriting – his signature always looked so regal and reminded me of the fancy script you'd find on the old one-pound notes back in those days. But something else always stuck in my mind about meeting Bill Nicholson: he always said 'thank you' after he had given you his autograph. Every time. It's these old-fashioned manners that you'll never see again from a modern manager. I mean, could you imagine any Premiership manager today ever strolling out of the ground, chatting to kids?

The season after the Double, Spurs won the 1962 FA Cup and in 1963 added the European Cup Winners' Cup to become the first British club to win a European trophy. Nicholson then won the FA Cup again with Tottenham in 1967, and then claimed the League Cup in 1971 and 1973 and the UEFA Cup in 1972, making him Tottenham Hotspur's most successful manager of all time. To commemorate the passing of such a great man, the club pulled out all the stops.

The Sunday and Monday after the Bolton game, which we lost 2–1, they kept the stadium doors open for supporters to pay their respects and to sign a book of condolence. And on Sunday, 7 November 2004, a fitting memorial was planned for the entire club, including the fans, to bid Bill Nicholson farewell.

The turnout was phenomenal. Players I knew from my childhood days, players I worked with, and the current stars of the day all turned out in their droves. I wouldn't have expected anything less, but it was a real testament to the man's iconic status among the footballing community that there were over 100 footballers at White Hart Lane that afternoon. I sat with Martin Jol and Hans Segers, but among us were players who went back as far as Bobby Smith, Cliff Jones and Ron Henry, who all played under Bill.

Among the legions of former players was Double-winning player Peter Baker, who must have flown especially from his home in South Africa to be there. Then you had

Chrissie Hughton, Stevie Perryman and Graham Roberts, and all the players from the current first-team squad. Most importantly, they let supporters and the public in too, as Bill Nicholson had known more than anyone that Spurs were a family team, and that the fans were key.

Jimmy Greaves later recalled in his speech that, when he was signed for Spurs, Bill Nicholson told him in no uncertain terms: 'When you run out in front of the crowd, these are the people that pay your wages. Their expectancy is high, their value of you is high, and their opinion of you is high. Do not let them down.'

Bill knew that the supporters were as much a part of the team as the players. And at his memorial, they opened the Paxton Road end and Spurs supporters were allowed to fill the entire bottom tier and, later, most of the upper.

They'd erected a big blue stage in front of the Paxton Road end, and the fans had left a wealth of tributes in front of the pitch, including shirts from through the ages, hundreds of scarves and a giant banner that read, 'Glory, Glory Tottenham Hotspur, 1961'. The advertising hoardings of the North and South Stands had been covered with a simple notice in Spurs navy blue that read: 'In loving memory Bill Nicholson OBE (1919–2004)'. The North West corner of the ground was given over to the family and friends of the late president, and a special ovation was given to Darkie, Bill's wife of over 60 years. This was a club in mourning.

Brian Alexander, the BBC Radio 5 Live presenter, took to the stage to begin proceedings and started by listing Bill's achievements in football, which took some time. The crowd were treated to a montage of images from the last two weeks, of the tributes that had poured in, accompanied by the beautifully haunting song 'Into the West' by Annie Lennox, which left many with tears in their eyes. But for me, it was the next song that made me fall apart: the Reverend Toni Smith from St Winifred's Church, Chigwell, introduced 'Abide With Me', and, as the violins began, I was instantly transported to Wembley Stadium, where the song is, of course, the traditional cup final hymn. I'd heard it sung there myself, but it was sung at Wembley three times in Bill Nicholson's era, each time before the great man lifted silverware.

I stood in my dark suit, quietly listening to this perfect requiem, which was a rare change for me, as a man who had worn a tracksuit nearly every day of his adult life. I remembered how much of an influence Bill Nicholson had been to me early in my career. When I joined the club, Bill had just been succeeded by Keith Burkinshaw, but was still very much involved in the club at all levels. As manager, general manager, ambassador, chief scout, or whatever title you gave him, Bill Nicholson knew the importance of the grass roots of the sport. Bill had his finger on the pulse, and he knew if the tea lady's kid was ill, or if we'd changed the type of paint we used to do the lines on the pitch.

His career had begun on 16 March 1936, when at the age

of 16 the young Bill Nicholson was invited to train at Tottenham Hotspur. After a month's trial, he was taken on as a ground-staff boy on £2 a week. So Bill knew what it was like to work at Tottenham Hotspur. He later signed as a full professional at the age of 18 and played a few matches for the first team before he joined the Durham Light Infantry on the outbreak of the Second World War in 1939. Years later, and Bill Nicholson still had as much time for the groundsman as he did for the team's centre forward, and it was being made to feel so special, even as lowly backroom staff, that empowered me to give so many years service to the club I loved. And it was in Bill's image I put in so many long hours, and dedicated so much of my life to his team.

There will never be another manager like Bill Nicholson. Take Jose Mourinho for instance: he wouldn't dream of getting involved in anything but coaching the team and perhaps transfers. Alex Ferguson perhaps comes closest to Bill, in that he has the same aura and unbending respect from everybody at his club. Bill's glorious Double, like Ferguson's Treble long after it, etched both men into the football history books, and, as I watched one player after another pay tribute at his memorial service, I contemplated fondly what a fine footballing side Bill created. When I watched matches at the Lane as a lad, the ball seldom went above head height. 'Up, back and through,' was Bill Nicholson's motto, and the ball would be played to the centre forward, who would control it and give it back, then run, and receive the ball back on the turn. It was deadly, and it was Bill Nicholson who pretty much invented it.

Steve Perryman was next to speak on stage, and the former club captain recounted the many adages that he had picked up from Bill Nicholson, including, 'When the game dies, make sure you come alive,' 'No spectators on the football pitch... people pay to do that!' and of course, 'If one ball goes back, the next goes through and forward.'

'Whenever I catch myself saying one of these on the sidelines,' admitted a tearful Steve Perryman, 'I think of Bill Nicholson, and now I always will.'

Black-and-white footage of the 1962 FA Cup semi-final came on to the screen as Cliff Jones and Jimmy Greaves climbed to the podium to offer their memories of Bill Nicholson. 'He would rarely congratulate a player,' remembered Cliff with a wry smile, 'and he always used to say, "A pat on the back is only two feet from being a kick up the arse!"' The Welshman recalled how Bill was always a stickler for detail, and revealed that, when he watched Cliff's debut for Spurs, Nicholson noticed that Cliff slipped while shooting in a dramatic 4–4 draw against Arsenal. Bill saw that the winger's studs were worn down, and he quipped after the game: 'The club will take care of your boots from now on.' You can see from this story that Bill was my kind of man.

The service concluded with the singing of 'Jerusalem', the Lord's Prayer and the release of one white dove for every year of Bill's life – 85 birds in all. As the dignitaries moved back towards the tunnel, more pictures were shown on the video screen and 'Glory Glory, Hallelujah' was played. It was both a memorable and a very solemn day, and afterwards there was a reception upstairs in the lounge for staff, players and friends. It felt much like a wake, such was the feeling of loss for a man who had done so much for the club. I feel so fortunate that I got to meet and later work for Bill Nicholson, and I look back on every encounter with fond memories. When I had my testimonial dinner on 21 October 1997, Bill was tragically too ill to make it, but sent an apologetic letter wishing me all the best. It was to be the last signature he would give me, 40 years after he first gave me an autograph as a boy. This final autograph, his hand unable to control the shakes, was wobbly, but still beautifully formed: the same beautiful signature I collected as a boy, stood waiting for him on the short road to the stadium, the road they later named after him in his honour.

CHAPTER 18

THE DREAM
IS OVER

When 20 uniformed police officers, plain-clothed coppers and scientific officers arrived at the hotel, it looked like a scene out of one of those detective movies. It was the night before our final game of the season of 2005/06, against West Ham United away, and the team had dined at the five-star Marriott Hotel in the Canary Wharf area of London's Docklands, in preparation for the big game. To win would mean qualification for the Champions League, to lose would mean being pipped to the post by our hated rivals Arsenal. It was certainly more than a life or death game, but something was afoot, and a very worried Tottenham Hotspur staff member had just reported that the team had been poisoned, and the police were called.

Was it an act of international terrorism? Or perhaps the Premiership's first ever case of professional sabotage?

'We have taken food samples from the hotel and we will pass them on to the appropriate authorities,' a Scotland Yard spokesman said, as Tottenham Hotspur's stomachs became a matter of national security. A policeman asked me as I walked through reception, 'Where were you between five and eight?' and I said, 'Primary school.' But I don't think he got the joke.

The first I knew of any trouble had been at nine o'clock on the Sunday morning. I'd loaded the van the night before, and was just leaving the training ground in Chigwell when I got a phone call. I was just about to swing on to the North Circular when I heard a very concerned voice in my ear. It was Martin Jol, who said, 'A couple of the lads have been ill in the night. Can you get me Lee Barnard's shirt, he'll have to play.' Martin then told me a couple of other reserve players who would now be likely to play, who were not even on the bench normally, so I put my foot down and sped back into the training ground. I raced into the kit room and grabbed all the shirts I'd been told to find, all high-numbered shirts belonging to the younger and more inexperienced players.

'I wonder what's happened?' I pondered as I got back in the van and tore down the road towards East London. It was after I'd been on the North Circular for a few miles, when my phone buzzed again, and, having slipped my hands-free kit into my ear once again, I heard an even more concerned Chris Hughton. 'You need to go back because another two players have gone down, we need some more shirts.' Blimey, I thought to myself, I might get a game myself, the way this is going.

By the time I finally got to Upton Park, I didn't know who was going to play. I set the dressing room up the best I could, and they arrived late for the 4pm kick-off, staggering in the door at gone half-two. A couple of the lads looked awful, and I remember Lee Barnard who was supposed to be playing was now ill himself and was sat, green to the gills, on the substitute bench. I knew this was terrible, as we hadn't put out the squad Martin Jol had selected for this important game on the Thursday previously. We were two or three players down, and Lee was behind me on the bench being violently sick into a bucket. He looked like death warmed up, and some of the players on the pitch looked just as bad.

On discovering the illness, the club had asked the Premier League to delay kick-off to give the players more time to recover, but we were denied. All six affected footballers played in the fixture, but it was not the preparation we needed to fight for that precious Champions League spot. Carl Fletcher of West Ham beat Paul Robinson with a soft 25-yard shot after just 11 minutes and, although Spurs pulled even, the Hammers struck again with a sweet strike on 80 minutes. Newton guided a pass to Nigel Reo-Coker and he back-heeled to Israeli Benayoun, who slipped past a struggling Michael Dawson before firing high past Robinson at the near post. The dream was over, and now Spurs were really sick.

Exhibit A in this detective drama became the lasagne the team ate on the Saturday night, which had reportedly left several players too weak to even stand. They took away the suspected dish and blood samples that had been taken by the team doctor, and the prime suspect was transported to Plaistow police station in East London, where it was kept overnight. The pasta dish, which had been prepared by Marriott chefs after a briefing from Spurs' diet and nutrition expert, was undergoing microbiological tests at independent government laboratories, as were the blood samples, but in the end it turned out it wasn't the lasagne at all, just a bug that had gone round the Spurs team.

Because you're a large group of men training in close quarters, bugs are part of the sport. Viruses happen. At Spurs we always took precautions, and should a player ever feel ill when he turns up to training, he reports to the club doctor, and they isolate him. He sits in a little room on his own, has his temperature taken, and when the lads are all out training the sick player is sent home so he doesn't infect the others. Sometimes you can't defend against airborne viruses. And you know, it's all 'if, buts and maybes', but you know that, even if you work on a building site or in an office, if you feel under the weather the last thing you want to do is perform. So imagine having to play bloody West Ham!

It wasn't just the players who were sick as parrots. At this point in my career I had become desperately unhappy with the job that I had once enjoyed for so many years. While in the past you used to get a day off after a game, and perhaps a day off in the week too, with the club getting into Europe it had become a seven-days-a-week job. Don't get me wrong, nothing could kill my love for Tottenham Hotspur, but I wasn't getting any younger, and this feeling of exhaustion had started around the time of manager Christian Gross, and had got steadily worse.

I think Christian Gross just wanted to come over and prove himself with a tough regime. When he moved to England in 1997, his family stayed behind in Switzerland, and because of that he became very, very football orientated and a real workaholic. Gross loved stats and he loved the buzz of the game but he was ridiculed by the press very early on. At that first press conference at White Hart Lane, Gross arrived late and had travelled by London Underground from Heathrow. He held his ticket aloft to prove it, and exclaimed, 'I want this to become my ticket to dreams. I came by Underground because I wanted to know the way the fans feel, coming to Spurs. I want to show that I am one of them.'

It was a bit cringey, and it went even further downhill from there.

A 6–1 defeat at home to Chelsea and a 4–0 away beating at lowly Coventry very early on made his start at Spurs less of a dream and more of a nightmare, but, to his credit, Gross didn't have the greatest team of players to work with. With what he did have, Gross was keen to make them into a 'proper team'. And that, for the Spurs players and staff, meant starting work at about 6.30 every morning. Christian was always, always at the training ground before me. He would make every home game feel like an away fixture by making the team check into a London hotel on a Friday night and making the players train in the hotel grounds before the game. Sundays off became a thing of the past, as win, lose or draw, we'd train Sunday morning at a local school, to 'warm down'. And while this wasn't easy for the players, it meant a full day of work for me too, looking after a gruelling seventh day of full training kit.

I don't think the new regime was particularly popular with the players, but it's like everything else: the manager makes the decisions and, whether you agree with it or not, you are paid to do a job. A *Guardian* journalist once claimed that 'Gross did not get on with anyone apart from Ramon Vega, the hapless Swiss defender who contrived to turn defensive mistakes into a slapstick art form.'

The intensity of my job became even more strenuous, because I would have to get up at silly o'clock on a match day and sort out a full training kit as well as the small matter of the match kit. It may sound like I'm complaining, but my job was already extremely demanding, as you've already gathered. What I had to do now was drive to the hotel on a Friday night, give the lads their training kits, go to the stadium and do whatever I had to do there, then drive back up to Enfield, pick up their training kit, then drive back to the stadium while they were having their pre-match meal. It became... ridiculous.

I had started to feel drained, but Spurs were my team and I put in the hours because I loved the club and I felt no one could do it like me. As the managers came and went – Graham, Hoddle and Santini – I began to get a little more disenchanted with every season. It was no coincidence that, after Bill Nicholson left, quite a lot of the staff at the club who had been there for donkeys years, who I knew and loved, began to leave. Like me, many had been there for 20-odd years, and I had a great affection for many of them. It was like a family, and without them the job changed. I wasn't losing love or faith with the club, it was just like Christian Gross's 'ticket to his dreams,' and I think mine had nearly expired.

Legendary Spurs and England goalkeeper Ted Ditchburn passed away at the age of 84 on 26 December 2005, contributing to the feeling that 2005/06 was a season of disappointments and sadness for Tottenham Hotspur. Martin Jol's battle for Champions League qualification had ended in failure after 'lasagne-gate', with Spurs finishing fifth behind Arsenal by just two points and qualifying for what felt like very much the consolation prize of entry to the UEFA Cup. I was exhausted. I had sadly separated from my wife in 2003 at the age of 49, and I was living in the family home alone, before I moved into my own place in 2004. I now had not one child, but two – Vikki, now 18, and Abbie, 11.

I'd been toying with the idea of life after the kit manager's job for about four years, but I was desperate to find a way to still stay involved at Spurs in some capacity. It was during a conversation with an old friend that I thought perhaps I might be able to make it as a players' agent, which seemed like a daunting, yet incredibly exciting prospect. Years previously I had met a gentleman called Robert Segal, a local chap who had come to watch Spurs training in the old days when you could just pop along to Page Street. We struck up a conversation, and a friendship ensued that would last decades. Rob was a barristers' clerk at the time, at a well-known place called Bedford Row Chambers and we had a lot in common, particularly our love for Tottenham Hotspur.

Over the years, as I progressed at Spurs, Rob's career also progressed and he became a football agent– it seemed like a natural move for someone with such an expert grasp of figures and the law, and a real passion for football. In the next few years, Rob would come to have a few Spurs players on his books, including the likes of Stephen Carr and Stephen Kelly, and later Paul Robinson. Soon, Robert was one of the biggest football agents in the country and had a stable of 20 to 30 players, so he was always down at Spurs, and sometimes, when my schedule allowed, we'd go to other games together. Well, I'd fancied working with Robert as a sort of a liaison officer for his agency, and I'd have been able to use my experience and contacts to bring new players to the business.

The problem was, Robert could only offer me a commission-only arrangement, and I had a big mortgage on my house. By now I was 52 and I felt that with one thing and another it wasn't the time to be taking risks. Then one day, I'd just had enough. The very idea of the end-of-season tour gave me the fear, and I was probably at my lowest ebb with the job. The pre-season tour, ordering in the 2000 pieces of kit, a manufacturer change to Puma and another gruelling campaign – including Europe – seemed too much for me to take, and it just felt like the right thing to do to approach the management and hand in my resignation.

It was a horrendous decision to make, but at the time it felt right. It was then that I began to think of Johnny Wallis, my old mentor, and how he carried on long after he loved the job. Johnny was 71 when he reluctantly left Tottenham Hotspur, and, while he gave everything he had to the club, I wondered if I had another purpose in life. After all, many players, coaches and staff had left Spurs to go on to better things, and I hoped that maybe I could do the same.

It was a long walk down that corridor at White Hart Lane to go and have that discussion with my superiors. It was a corridor I had painted in the 1970s as a member of the ground staff, and over the years it had since been licked with a hundred fresh coats of paint. A thousand players had walked this walk: Bill Nicholson, Alan Mullery, Dave Mackay, Gary Mabbutt, Gary

Lineker, Cliff Jones, Pat Jennings and another army of hopefuls, all praying for a career at Tottenham as long as mine. They say your life flashes before your eyes at the end, and Tottenham was my life. With every footstep I became more emotional as the memories floated back to me: Ricky Villa, swerving through those City defenders, Gascoigne's free-kick, the tears and the ecstasy and the glory.

My testimonial was held at the Royal Lancaster Hotel in West London, which is where we'd celebrated the 1991 Cup Final win. There were 250 people there, and all the first-team squad including manager Gerry Francis on the top table. Some of the older players from my past had turned up, including Stevie Perryman and Chris Hughton. It was unusual for a member of staff to have a testimonial, in fact, only one other non-player was given a testimonial in living memory, and that was my predecessor, Johnny Wallis. So to be given this honour was such a proud moment. For all those times I hoped that I might achieve a small part of the respect that Johnny received from his peers, I felt that by getting a testimonial I had maybe achieved it.

We had a fabulous evening. The comedian was fantastic; he wore a cracking black-and-white striped shirt, and as he walked on to the stage he picked out Les Ferdinand in the crowd and said, 'Remember this?' pointing at his striped outfit. 'This was when you scored goals, son!' He brought the house down.

Unfortunately, David Ginola couldn't make it, and he was gutted he couldn't attend but sent me a lovely note apologising. So did Bill Nicholson, who was too ill to be there as I mentioned, and he wrote: 'Due to my circumstances, I cannot attend, but I wish you the very best.' I was so emotional when I read that note.

On my testimonial, I had served 22 years, and even then I wouldn't have believed I'd do another seven before throwing in the towel.

My successor was Steve Dukes, who had been my trusty assistant for some time. Steve had done a bit of kit management at Watford, and more at QPR. He'd helped out around the ground for a while and was watching me and taking notes. When Steve got an opportunity to come in as my assistant, I pushed for him to get it, because he was trustworthy and he always asked me questions. I remembered back to when I was assisting Johnny Wallis, and I'd be asking all these daft questions... 'Why do you do that to the collars?' or 'Why do you fold them like that?' I liked Steve, and when he picked my brains, like I had with Johnny, I shared the secrets of life as Tottenham's kit man. When I left, I told Steve, 'Whatever you need, just ring me and I'll take you through it.' But, although I could tell Steve at what temperature to wash a home shirt, there was no way I could prepare him for the reality of the job. I supposed he'd find out along the way – that it's the best job in the world for a Spurs fan.

But for me, what was next? What do you do after 29 years of Tottenham Hotspur? Well, instead of trying to become a burgeoning football agent at the age of 52, I decided to do what I knew best, and stay directly in football. So I went to work for an ex-Spurs and Colchester player, Steve Grenfell, who had a coaching school in Enfield. I had my coaching badges, accrued during my time at Spurs, so I went to work full-time for him for about six months, doing curriculum sports coaching in schools, which was absolutely tremendous for me.

I loved coaching the kids and, having two of my own and having looked after a raft of young Spurs boys, it was great to go into schools and teach 'multi-sports'. I'd teach tennis, rugby, cricket – all sports to all ages, and then manage the after-school club too. For the first time I was working a normal day: 8 till 5, and loving every hour of it. That was a fun summer, spent joyously watching children get their first grasp of football, and it felt so different to spend some time away from White Hart Lane and the training ground.

Of course, when the season came around, I began to feel a horrible yearning in my stomach that I can't quite explain. For three decades, I had lived and breathed every second of Tottenham, from behind the scenes. The access I had to the club, the transfer rumours and every single detail – from the colour of the new away strip to the latest Academy players who were rumoured to be the next Ledley King – to have that suddenly taken away, to be suddenly missing from that world, made me feel like a fish out of water. No, it was worse, it felt like grieving.

Of course, there was a bigger problem: that I wasn't earning the money that I required to cover my outgoings on my mortgage, and I had two young daughters to look after. The only way I could make my money up was to coach with the schools during the week, and at amateur clubs on a Saturday. But then all of a sudden I realised that the reason I left Spurs was to get my life back, and now I was working all the hours under the sun again.

Then, one day right out of the blue I got a call from a man who said he worked for Saracens, the rugby club. Laird Budge, a former assistant of mine, had recommended me for a job at the club. When Laird left Spurs,, he became the kit man at Barnet Town under Ray Clemence, and I'd spoken to him a few times on the phone, as he picked my brains about the kit job. Well, Laird went on to work at Hatfield University, coaching their football side, and they shared a training ground with Saracens, who as it turned out, had a vacancy for a kit manager. 'Well,' I thought, 'I'm not losing anything by going to speak to them,' even though I knew nothing about rugby other than they play with odd-shaped balls!

My interview was with the fitness coach, the assistant manager and the team manager, and then I was invited back for a second interview with all three of them, plus the head coach. They told me Saracens were planning on upgrading their backroom staff, with a view to becoming a serious contender as a top English rugby team. Then they asked me to sum up my career at Tottenham. And I just said, 'How long have you got?'

CHAPTER 19
ODD-SHAPED BALLS

Before joining Saracens, I'd only ever seen rugby on the television. I would only tune in to the big England Internationals, or perhaps the odd big final, because football kept me busy enough. To me, the rules of rugby were so confusing, and it was a really daunting task to learn an entirely new sport at the age of 52 to be able to do the job. At times, it felt like studying for a degree, or perhaps doing 'the knowledge' as a London cab driver. But as well as learning a fundamental lesson in the rules, I quickly gained a respect for the technical aspect of the sport, something I had completely underestimated.

Technical plays in professional rugby are so intricate that it's mind-blowing. When I watched my first training match at Saracens, I saw a lineout – you know, when they all jump up for what looks like a throw-in – and I just assumed that whoever jumped highest got the ball. But I soon found out that there are a plethora of calls and different variations of who jumps when and an infinite number of permutations. And when they scrummage, it's not a gang of blokes having a ruck, it's a science.

Saracens have got a specialist scrum coach, Cobus Visage, and, if you watch a live scrum session, you'll see the players taking on each other or even against special machines – it's magnificent. When I told my Spurs mates how much work goes into rugby training, they didn't believe it. And now that I understand and respect it, rugby is extremely exciting.

At my job interview, I'd been told by the Director of Rugby, Alan Gaffney, that Saracens had finished just tenth in the league the season before. 'We want to end this losing streak,' said Gaffney. 'And you can change whatever you want to make behind the scenes a more professional atmosphere.'

So, we negotiated the hours and wages, and I took the job. But I had no idea what I was walking into. I quickly learned that the team had not had a proper kit man for years. It was just done by the lads or the coaches and, unbelievably, every day after training the players would take their own kit away and wash it at home! I imagined asking David Ginola or Edgar Davids to wash their own kit! What's more, we didn't even have our own training ground; instead, we shared facilities in Hatfield, but we could only train there three times a week and often we'd turn up the day before a game and be told by the groundsman that we couldn't train at all.

I began to yearn for the posh training ground and facilities that George Graham had built for me at Tottenham Hotspur. I soon realised that the kit situation at Saracens was completely unmanageable: if a player turned up having forgotten an item of kit, they'd have to drive to Bramley Road, a 40-minute journey, which was ludicrous. I told the bosses at Saracens that I'd need to completely overhaul the entire training ground and kit system, and I was pleased when Edward Griffiths, CEO of the club, gave me his full backing. 'Do what you have to, Roy, just keep us in the picture,' they said. It was then that I got to work, and when we moved to Harpenden, to Old Albanians, that I began to build my own little empire.

I managed to find a funny little room inside the training ground, which was no more than a broom cupboard, and, with some DIY, I fashioned a miniature version of my storeroom at Spurs Lodge. There was a kitchen where the staff used to make a brew, so I moved in some industrial-size washing machines and made my laundry. Then I moved all the computer servers out of another small room, brought in the heat transfer equipment for printing the players' names and numbers – and I was in business. The minute the last shelf was erected and the team's famous black-and-red shirts were piled up high to the ceilings, I sat down on my little chair, made a cuppa, and wondered if, by rebuilding my Spurs dressing room, albeit on a much smaller scale, I could rebuild the life I'd had at White Hart Lane. Could I ever feel the same way about Saracens that I felt about Tottenham Hotspur?

As I've said, I'd become such a big part of Spurs, and the club had become a big part of me: White Hart Lane had been my home for the last 30 years. For the first few weeks after I left, everything felt all right on the surface. But the first home game I missed at White Hart Lane felt very strange. It just seemed wrong for me to be home on a Saturday morning, and I felt lost without my Spurs. I remember I woke up with the game on my mind. I was due to coach some schoolchildren on a playing field in Cheshunt, but, as I got in the car and started the engine, my mind began to drift. Would Ledley be starting? I wondered. What would Robbie Keane be doing right now? Perhaps checking the size label of his shirt as he always did, slipping the shinpads that I'd lovingly made for him inside his brand-new socks. I found myself automatically on my way to White Hart Lane, driving towards the ground as I'd done every Saturday for decades. When I realised, I pulled over, and felt an unmistakable lump in my throat. There was a giant Spurs-shaped hole in my heart.

Joining Saracens helped to heal that wound, as I was welcomed into the club like one of the family. Rugby is a very close-knit society, and soon I felt like I'd been at the club forever. I remember my first match: in the opening minute one of our lads was clattered and his nose exploded all over his away shirt. It was awful, the kind of injury that would stop play in football and end in hospitalisation for the player. I immediately dashed into the kit room to get a blood shirt, but, when I came back out, play had resumed, and the injured player was back on the field, getting stuck in like nothing had happened. They'd just patched him up and plugged his nose up and on he ran again, back for more action! I was amazed.

As the saying goes, 'Rugby is a game for hooligans played by gentlemen,' and I can only speak as I find. On my first away game with Saracens, I was starting to load the skips full of kit into the team coach, which was hard work. Suddenly, the team were released from a tactical meeting and filed out into the car park, where they saw me lifting the giant skips. They all, to a man, picked up a bag and a skip and helped me put the stuff in, something a footballer would never dream of doing. The only team I had experienced who had got stuck in like that was Liverpool in the 1980s. I had travelled to Anfield and got to the ground nice and early as usual to lay the kit out. Ian Rush was injured, so he was at the ground for treatment at 9.30am and, as I was unloading the coach, he said, 'Morning, mate.' Then he asked about the skips: 'Do these need to go in?' Next, I watched in wonder as Ian helped me on about five journeys to carry all the Spurs kits into the dressing room. Doug Livermore and Ray Clemence later told me that that was the Liverpool way, and I was mightily impressed.

Life at a rugby club was certainly an eye-opener at times. Especially my first pre-season tour in 2006, when we flew to Portugal, to a training camp called Browns. The place had superb facilities, a purpose-built gym, swimming pool, training pitches, a sand pitch for heavy running, and even a basketball court. We went to the beach to train for two days, and special strength and conditioning coaches arranged a gruelling circuit on the beach. This included wrestling and grappling, then boxing, running, then finally into the sea to swim round a member of staff in a flotation jacket, and then run back up the beach. Plenty of footballers wouldn't have done it! But for the rugby boys, there wasn't a single moan, and even the non-swimmers tackled the punishing course.

The social side of the sport was also new to me. Back at the hotel pool after training, the team had set up an impromptu 'court hearing'. The team captain was the judge, and the rest of the players were judge and jury. Any player or member of staff could be called to stand trial for some kind of 'crime'. It could be bushy eyebrows, being late for dinner, having a bad haircut or whatever, and the committee would sentence you! I was terrified, as I am no big drinker.

I was caught out early on by a game of 'left-hand drinking only', and had to down a bottle of beer before being sentenced to drink from a bowl of mystery liquid… simply for being the new boy. I had to scoop into a bowl of what looked like water, and down a full cup. Well, it nearly knocked my head off! It was a mixture of every type of white spirit behind the bar: vodka, Bacardi, gin… it was rocket fuel! I was really in trouble.

Finally, I had to sit on what they called 'The Bus' with ten players sat on two rows of five chairs. The first person had to neck a bottle of beer, stick it on his head, then the person behind him did the same, and it was a race to beat the other side of the bus. We lost three times, which meant that as a non-drinker I'd downed a bottle of lager, necked a cup of spirits and swallowed three more bottles of beer. By this stage I was really rocking and rolling, but I was shocked to find out that this little ceremony was just the warm-up for a full night of boozing down in the port! I got back to my room to change, and it was like I was on a boat. Just half an hour later, I told Nigel – the only teetotal one, in charge of driving the bus down to the marina – 'I've got to go home.'

Nigel took me straight back to the hotel and I was asleep at 9.15pm! The next morning I woke up at 7.30 and I had a mouth like Gandhi's flip-flop. I was in a terrible pickle. So I had a cold shower and set up the training kit, but, when the lads came in, they looked brand new! They were bright eyed and bushy tailed, and, when I staggered down to watch them train, their session was so intensive it made me feel sick just watching them. Rugby boys are a different breed, and it was at Saracens that I learned how close a team could be.

Saracens' lock forward, Mouritz Botha, has got his own leisurewear brand, and on the front of the T-shirts is printed: 'There's a lot of love in this team'. And at Saracens, there really is. Paul Gustard, Brendan Venter and the boys aren't just a team, we are more a family. We've got another T-shirt that says 'Raised By Wolves', as there's a real pack mentality at Saracens. Things like that, I'd love to take back to Tottenham Hotspur. When I first started at Spurs, there was a bit of a social element to the team: Graham Roberts, Stevie Perryman and a few players would all meet in a pub in Cheshunt after the game, but ever since then I can't remember that happening. I'm not recommending any team starts going out boozing, but what I'll say about Saracens is that the strength of our social life together means that, if there's any animosity, it's dealt with properly. I've seen amazing tear-ups on the training field: full-scale blows and almighty punch-ups. And never once have they walked off the field anything less than best buddies; they'll have a beer or a coffee at lunchtime and it's done and dusted.

The arrival of South African Brendan Venter as the head coach in 2009 sparked major controversy at Saracens, because the growing number of South Africans to the squad caused the club to be strongly criticised in the media, as we were seen to be swaying away from being an English club. It didn't feel like that on the inside, and we quickly embarked upon a ten-match unbeaten run at the start of the domestic season, which included a win over London Irish at Twickenham in the London Double Header, beating Northampton at Wembley, and even rugby giants London Wasps and Bath.

And the South African element was also a valuable asset for the club, as it meant a strong connection to a country where rugby is a major passion. It was also a country close to my heart, after that pre-season trip with Tottenham Hotspur that affected me so deeply. Some of our directors at Saracens are South African and today we've got six or seven players. I'd often ask questions about the shanty towns that I had visited that day when we drove to the outskirts of the townships with Robbie Keane, Jamie Redknapp and the rest of the Spurs boys. I told them I found it difficult to comprehend the poverty, and they told me, 'It's our way of life, Roysie, but we're doing what we can to help.'

I'd been so frustrated that I couldn't go right into the township with Spurs, not because I could have solved their problems, but because I'd had a glimpse into what terrible problems those children have out there. It had really affected me, because of my love for children. Not just my own kids or the ones I'd coached, but all children.

In South Africa, there are kids who have HIV from the day they are born. People talk about fate, and they say that, no matter how painful things are, they happen for a reason. I always found it difficult to comprehend this, as I had struggled most of my life to come to terms with my father passing away when I was 18. Why did that have to happen? They say that, in times of grieving, that loss is simply fate's way of making room for something new. It was only when I left Tottenham Hotspur that I began to understand that – because at Saracens I had got my life back, and more.

On a pre-season tour to South Africa, as the plane dipped below the thick white clouds and began to circle Cape Town International Airport, the entire Saracens family looked out of the windows at the sprawling city below: a foreign land to most of them, and 'home' to the rest. For me, I had unfinished business here, and, as the throttle roared and the plane sank lower towards to the ground, the sprawling townships came into focus far below us, like an epic expanse of poverty. This would be more than just a pre-season rugby tour for me.

Our coach, Brendan Venter, a doctor in his other life, is responsible for the formation and upkeep of an HIV clinic in a disadvantaged area of South Africa, and as the *Sunday Times* once wrote of him: 'You see the other side of the man when he is taking people aside and telling them that they are HIV positive.'

Brendan organised a trip right into the beating heart of the township, miles past the areas where a normal tour guide would deem 'safe'. I saw first-hand the conditions that these families are living in: a squalid dump with no electricity and no sanitation, just a trench between each row of houses that filled slowly with excrement each day. How these people actually live is quite harrowing.

'We're going to build this young man a new house,' Brendan announced, after we had walked sombrely through a row of particularly shabby huts, all of us dressed in our official Saracens outfits. We met and shook hands with a very grateful young man, who the translator revealed had lost both of his parents to HIV, and who was living alone in a shack that was falling down. The boy just smiled a wide smile of disbelief as we began carrying in timber and tools and all the materials to build him a proper house. It didn't take long to demolish his own house. You could have leaned on it and it would have collapsed. It didn't take long for him to move out either, as his belongings were simply a table and a chair.

We spent the afternoon building a proper house for our man in the searing heat, swatting flies from our faces as we hammered nails and sawed lengths of wood. And when we finished, the lad was so happy. But then he looked at the pile of scrap metal and corrugated iron on the floor, and asked one of the South African players what we were going to do with all the scrap. So next, we rebuilt his old home, properly this time, and his little mate moved in next door! It was so satisfying, but Brendan wasn't finished yet.

We travelled further into the township, to a compound for women sufferers of HIV. Researchers estimate that 10.9% of all South Africans were living with HIV in 2008, and the disease kills as many as 14,783 every year, many of them young women. The compound we visited was full of women who had either been born with the disease or contracted it. We were to rebuild their garden, which was in a bit of a state. The Saracens boys quickly got to work, levelling it and building walls out of earth. Next, we brought in lots of flowers, and planted them. If only you could have seen our massive rugby boys delicately bedding in flowers in the garden, under the watchful eyes of these women.

Even the female staff that worked at the compound were HIV positive, yet their outlook on life was amazing. We spent the whole day there, fully landscaping their garden, and in the hot South African sun it was a hell of a task. I remember standing back when we finished, and sweat was pouring down my back. But this was such satisfying work. Sometimes you get so embedded in your world – the endless cycle of training kit washes and match days – that you forget how relatively meaningless it all is compared to the hardships some people on the planet endure. At last I felt like I was really doing something.

'You must come inside and let us feed you,' one of the women told us sweetly, and soon we were inside the compound, and the ladies were serving us their traditional meal of rice and vegetables. They'd cooked it especially for us, but to be honest it wasn't at all appetising. I could tell the lads all felt the same, but, to a man, we polished it off. There was no way we wouldn't finish it, as this was their way of saying thank you for our hard work. Then, after dinner, when every plate was clear, a dozen of the women stood up in traditional dress and sang a South African song for us. If you take the feeling produced by walking out at Wembley behind Gazza and Terry Venables to a chorus of Spurs fans singing, and multiply it by ten, you wouldn't be half the way there. It was the most beautiful thing I've ever heard.

Their voices were so hauntingly beautiful, and, as I glanced down the row of muscle-bound rugby players, each of them was struggling to choke back tears. There were tears in my eyes too, as these ladies finished their song, and we politely applauded.

It was a tremendous, life-changing experience that tour, and life with Saracens would get better and better for me, as the team went from strength to strength. Soon after I joined we reached two cup semi-finals, including the Heineken Cup at Worcester, where we were defeated by Munster, who are like the Atlético Madrid of rugby. That was my first big rugby experience at the club, and it was just as nerve-wracking as any Spurs cup final. Saracens had lost all of their six previous semi-final games in all competitions in the last three years, and the club were desperate to get to a final to prove that we were a top force in British rugby. Glen Jackson, our Kiwi fly-half, had played in six losing semi-finals himself, and in 2010, our semi against mighty Northampton, would be one of his last games for Saracens, and his last chance to get to a major final with the club. Everyone was up for it.

This was such an exciting time for the club, for, being such a close-knit family, everyone from the secretary to the turnstile boys was desperate for us to succeed. And in an almighty clash, we beat Northampton 21–19 in the last minute, the winning kick scored by none other than Glen Jackson, who heroically converted Schalk Brits' driving-maul try. Saracens would be in our first final since 1998, and the supporters and players were ecstatic. I felt like I did in 1991 when Spurs beat Arsenal in the FA Cup semi-final. Alas, Saracens were beaten in the final. The 2010 Guinness Premiership Final at Twickenham on 29 May pitted us against the eight-time and reigning English Champions, Leicester Tigers, and, although we were narrowly beaten, Saracens had proved that we were a top-flight club and we finished a respectable third place in the Guinness Premiership, just four points behind Leicester. It was a huge achievement.

Days after the final, I celebrated my wedding reception at the Old Albanians ground in Harpenden, that, like the Saracens team, I had come to call home. My new bride, Alison, and my two daughters looked fantastic, and, as I reflected on my life, I realised that it had become true what they say: that, when you lose one thing, it just makes room for something else in your life. And as I looked out over the pristine rugby pitches I realised I was happy once again. Of course, people often ask me if I'd ever go back to Tottenham Hotspur, and I sometimes say that I wish I'd never left. Of course, I deeply regretted my decision, but such is life.

I still managed to get to Spurs home games when my Saracens commitments allowed, and I had watched with glee as we qualified for the Champions League. Of course, it's not the same watching from up in West Stand, seemingly miles away from my 'usual position' in the dugout. I wondered how it would feel watching Spurs run out under those electric floodlights, the team all in white and in Europe once again, like they were when I was a wide-eyed boy in the stands. Today, when I visit White Hart Lane, I often walk past Bill Nicholson Way, and out of habit sometimes I linger a little longer than I should, in case I see a player coming out. Would I return to Tottenham Hotspur? Well, I never say never. But for now I'll just walk past those famous gates, where I'm once again on the outside looking in with wonderment, on Tottenham Hotspur, the club I love.